AVAILABLE LIGHT
PHOTOGRAPHY

by

H. M. KINZER

UNIVERSAL PHOTO BOOKS

Publishers of Fine Books in the Photographic Field

PREFACE

This book is an introduction to a special kind of photography. It is not intended to be a basic handbook of photography itself, but is for those people who may have read one or two general introductory books, and want to know where to go from there. This book tells how to make available-light pictures, a kind of picture not covered in "first readers" of photography.

Various chapters in this book will tell you about the cameras, films, meters and developers used in available-light photography. All of the book is devoted to handling this equipment and available-light subjects; it tells you and gives you many examples of exposure settings and how pictures are taken.

You will find repetition in this book: the kind of repetition that helps you learn. For instance, you may read about making portraits in the section that deals with the technical details of equipment and exposures; you will also read more about portraits in a chapter that tells you what it is like to work with an available-light camera in a typical portrait situation. In like manner, you will read about photographing children in two different sections — or night pictures, or office pictures. Each time the subject is presented from a slightly different approach, or with a different emphasis.

The author has chosen to include as many examples of available-light photography as possible. This has meant some sacrificing of what the trade calls "nuts-and-bolts" pictures — hands holding cameras, hands manipulating exposure meters, etc. The author feels that this ground has been too well covered in general introductory photographic texts to necessitate repetition here.

The pictures in this book are not presented as the best available light pictures obtainable. That would be presumptuous, and it would not be highly desirable either. It is much more instructive to look at a book full of pictures that are on a par with the best you can make when you finish reading this book, than to be shown scores of big-name professional shots, most of them out of reach of the average amateur. Thus, many photographs in this book were taken by amateurs, some by contest winners, and a few by working professionals. All photographs were chosen on the basis of:

1. Quality, which is high enough to inspire any would-be available-light photographer.

2. Subject matter, to reflect the kind of available-light situations you are most likely to encounter.

3. Equipment, to show results and the methods of working with the simplest as well as the more complicated cameras.

It is hoped that both the text and pictures of this book will help you to take good available-light pictures, choose and use available-light equipment, and use proper developing procedures.

New York, N. Y.   H. M. KINZER

ACKNOWLEDGMENTS

The author is indebted to *Popular Photography*, and to its editor Bruce Downes, for permission to use its research facilities and some photographs from its annual International Picture Contest.

A special debt is acknowledged to Bob Schwalberg, contributing editor of *Popular Photography*, a working photojournalist, and an untiring experimenter, whose efforts have served mightily to push back the boundaries of available-light photography in the past decade. The author has relied heavily on the reports of his research.

Among the many photographers who made their photographs available, I wish to express my gratitude to the following: Maynard Frank Wolfe, Pat Caulfield, Harvey Shaman, Bob Schwalberg, Albert Gruen, Diane Pattou, Arthur Goldsmith, P. E. Guerrero, William Noyes, John Durniak, Michael Aleshire, Martin Dain, and Joseph P. Fesce.

The book was technically edited by L. Jules Levitan, whose years of experience as both a still and motion picture cameraman and exhibitor, as well as his work as author, designer of photographic equipment, and instructor in photography, has enabled him to be of much help in checking all the technical facts in this book.

NOTE ON THE THIRD EDITION

In the preparation of this revised edition, the author has relied heavily on the wise and friendly collaboration of Bill Pierce, a contributing technical editor of *Popular Photography*. He has built skilfully on the foundation laid by Bob Schwalberg, and judiciously chosen film and developer combinations from today's bewildering array that are best suited to available-light shooting. He has also written a valuable post-script on "How to Determine Your Own Exposure Indexes and Developing Times." He and Ted Runge have also contributed new pictures for this edition.

CONTENTS

NOTE

Several of the photographs in this book were made on Kodak Super-XX film, which was withdrawn for sale shortly after the first edition appeared. Its recommended ASA rating was 100, or somewhat faster than the present Plus-X. Exposure data in captions of Super-XX pictures can thus be useful if considered to relate to a film speed between that of Plus-X and Tri-X.

The new improved Plus-X is still officially rated by Kodak at 80 ASA, but the manufacturer points out that this allows for a "safety factor" to prevent underexposure, and suggests a higher rating be used. Experience indicates Plus-X should be rated at least at 160.

CHAPTER 1

WHAT AVAILABLE LIGHT IS

- - - and What It Isn't

What Is Available Light?

This is a term you will find in no dictionary, and probably in no "recognized" glossary of photography. It is an expression that has taken its meaning from experience, and has gained authority through use. There are two other terms which are sometimes used to mean the same thing: "existing light," and "natural light" — although the latter has also been widely used to mean simply daylight.

Available light is the illumination that is present in a situation for purposes of picture-making. Available-light photography is the taking of pictures under conditions other than good daylight — without using artificial light sources such as flash, flood, and spotlights.

Pioneers in the use of available-light technique were men like Dr. Erich Salomon, whose camera chronicled the political and diplomatic life of the Twenties and Thirties with an unmatched sense of reality; and Alfred Eisenstaedt, whose professional career began in 1929, and who functions today as a mainstay of *Life* magazine's photographic staff.

Why Available Light?

There is no reason why you should not use flashbulbs or floodlights when existing light is not sufficient, if you prefer them. There

H. M. Kinzer

LIGHT QUANTITY VERSUS
LIGHT QUALITY. This pair
of pictures illustrates the
difference in quality between available light and floodlight.
The top picture of singer Mary McCoy was made in a booth
at the National Photo Show, where light was comparable
to that in an average living room. It was shot with a 35-mm
camera at 1/25 second, f/2. The picture on the right, made
when Mary stepped out on the stage, was shot with the
same camera at 1/50 second, f/5.6. The photographer was
able to go on the stage to take exposure meter readings in
advance. Note how the natural light gives excellent modeling to the features in the portrait, while the brilliant photoflood lighting on the stage blanked out all the highlights in
the face. Both negatives were printed straight, on the same
contrast grade of paper.

are two big reasons why professionals and serious amateurs are turn-ing more and more to the available-light technique whenever they can use it:

1. To preserve the quality of the natural situation,
   and to avoid intruding on it.
2. For ease and convenience.

It's True To The Situation

The first reason, of course, is most important. Whenever we can make good pictures in any situation without using harsh flash or glaring flood, and without drawing attention to our presence, we have an advantage. For example, you have seen a shot of a group of businessmen bent over a table, apparently engrossed in their work, but photographed with the harsh glare of flash so that they look a little like escapees in the beam of a prison searchlight.

On the other hand, you have seen (especially if you have looked at some of *Fortune* magazine's excellent picture stories on the business world) a photograph of another group of executives, working without apparent awareness of the photographer, in the natural light of their office.

This latter picture conveyed a much more accurate and revealing impression of *the way people really were* and *the way the place looked.* This is the essence of the reasons for using available-light technique. You see, it is not only the quality of the light that makes the difference, it is also the available-light technique that makes it possible for the photographer to work without disturbing the situa-tion. Instead of being a stage-director (as he often must with elabor-ate lighting setups) the photographer can be a kind of participating player, and his camera can watch from "inside" rather than remain-ing a menacing eye from "outside."

It's Simpler And Convenient

The advantage of ease and convenience is quite obvious, though less important — for a serious photographer's code is "Get the picture!" no matter what obstacles arise. In principle, a working cameraman is willing to carry armloads of equipment — even station wagons full of it — and hire an assistant to set it up for him, if he feels he can get a better picture that way. However, if he can confront an assignment with nothing but a six-inch-long camera and a pocketful of film, he will be happier, freer in movement, and a lot less conspicuous.

One of the nation's greatest industrial photographers is a man who was trained in newspaper picture-taking — cut his eye teeth on a 4x5 press camera, so to speak. His superior big-camera work got him his job and his well deserved reputation. Just a few years ago, he began to use a 35-mm camera and available-light technique. Soon he found himself using it more often than any other. Today he is happiest when he approaches a situation that requires no flash, no lighting setups, no large negatives — and he sees to it that an increasing number of his jobs fit that description!

The relationship between a man, his camera, and his subject is something that ought not to be tampered with or "arranged." And a good photographer's time is too valuable to be spent on anything except the making of good pictures.

Why a Special Technique?

If it's just a matter of taking pictures under weak light, why not simply grab a high-speed lens, load up with a high-speed film, and "soup it up" in a high-speed developer — and hope for the best? Why a whole *system?*

Because . . .

— It's not merely a question of speed, but of quality at the same time.

— Fast lenses are unnecessary for many available-light shots.

— Ordinary films are sometimes better than high-speed ones.

— "Souping-up" is not necessarily the way to increase speed.

— You don't get "the best" by simply hoping for it.

The success of available-light photography depends on every step from the conception and planning of the picture to the presentation of the finished print. At every level there are right and wrong ways of proceeding, and not necessarily the same right and wrong ways that apply to other kinds of photography.

4

Vito Fiorenza, from Popular Photography Picture Contest

LITTLE GIRLS OF SICILY. By available-light photography, the natural quality of this church scene has been preserved, because the photographer and his basic equipment did not intrude. Fiorenza exposed for the tones of the faces, allowing the bright background to blank out — which also helped to set off the foreground figures better. He was using a twin-lens reflex and Super-XX film, and exposed at 1/25 second at f/3.5.

5

Al Francekevich, from Popular Photography Picture Contest

FACE IN THE SUBWAY. The distinctive quality of this shot is in the reality of the mood and expression, caught by unobtrusive handling of the camera, which was a Rolleicord. For this scene of a subway running above ground, an exposure of 1/10 second at f/4 on Plus-X was required; the window areas were greatly overexposed, but there is good detail in the face.

The problem is not just to get a recognizable image of the subject, but to get one that is as satisfactory as it could have been made in any other way — and more faithful to the subject matter.

If you are to develop an appreciation for this kind of photography, you must have other gods than fine grain and razor sharpness. You must also bow to something called verisimilitude—a big word that means "the appearance of truth." Today, with reasonable care and aptitude, you can get all the sharpness and fine grain you need. But the "appearance of truth" is hard to achieve.

The Elements of the System

1. A small camera with a fast lens.

2. A film-and-developer combination that offers maximum working emulsion speed at optimum quality.

3. An eye for reality.

Element No. 1 is subject to economic considerations. If you can't afford the finest and fastest, something less will do as well.

For Elements No. 2 and 3, there are no alternatives.

Typical Available-Light Cameras.

(A)   35-mm RANGEFINDER-VIEWFINDER TYPE. These can have the fastest lenses (ranging from f/4.5 to f/1.4), focal-plane shutters with a wide range of speeds, take a 20 or 36 exposure film load, and take interchangeable lenses. Some have rapid film advances. Shown is a Leica M-3 (courtesy E. Leitz, Inc.).

(B)   SINGLE-LENS REFLEX, 35-mm. Viewing is directly through the taking lens by means of a mirror and prism system, focal-plane shutters usually having a wide range of speeds, takes interchangeable lenses and extension tubes for extreme close-ups. This is the Heiland Pentax H-3 (courtesy Heiland Photo Products Div., Minneapolis-Honeywell Co.).

(C)   TWIN-LENS REFLEX. The image is viewed on groundglass through separate lens; most have 120 or 127 roll film taking 12 square pictures on a roll. The lenses are usually f/3.5, though some are f/2.8. There is a cocking mechanism coupled to the film advance knob or crank. This is the Automatic Rolleiflex (courtesy Burleigh Brooks Co.).

CHAPTER 2

EQUIPMENT AND MATERIALS

Cameras, Films and Accessories

What Kind of Camera Do You Need?

If you own a camera now, no matter what kind it is, it is probably adequate for some kinds of available light. However, if it is an extremely simple one — a box or folding model with few or no adjustments — you may want to get a better one. Here is a guide to your choice.

Naturally, a camera with a wide lens opening and slow shutter speeds will enable you to encompass more of the available-light situations than one that does not have them. But the simplest camera, even the most reasonably priced box, can make pictures under "moderately poor" conditions, such as those called Class I in *Chapter 4.*

A moderately priced camera, with a maximum lens aperture of $f/4.5$ or $f/3.5$ and shutter speeds down to $1/10$ or $1/5$ of a second, can make good pictures under the "average" conditions described in Class 2.

For the "abysmal" lighting situations of Class 3 the fastest lenses are almost essential. These can be expensive. But you will find that there are some models with $f/2.8$ and even $f/2$ lenses at moderate prices — beginning around $50, new. Incidentally, don't overlook the possibility of getting a good used camera from a reputable dealer. It's a way of getting into the fast-lens bracket on a budget.

While you're deliberating about how fast a lens to get, remember this: with today's new films and developers, an $f/3.5$ lens can easily do what it took an $f/2$ lens to do just a few years ago. A fast lens *plus* a new fast film simply means that now you can take pictures that would have been totally impossible before.

A wide aperture has one more advantage in the kind of situations in which you will usually work with available light. When you have read about the *Basics of Photography* in *Chapter 3*, you will understand how aperture controls *depth of field* — that is, the distance between the nearest and farthest parts of your subject that are in sharp focus. When you "stop down" (use a large f-number), you get everything sharp from a few feet to infinity. You might want to do this for an over-all shot of a large gathering. But more often, as in candid portraiture or snapping babies in the nursery or children at play, you will want to *single out* a subject or part of it, to avoid the distracting objects in the background or foreground. For this purpose, the wider you can open the aperture, the better. So we can say that the "faster" the lens, the more selectivity it gives you in your field of focus.

What About Film Size?

Because available-light technique is usually synonymous with inconspicuous, unobtrusive camera operation, you will want a small camera. This means, generally speaking, one of two film sizes: 35-mm perforated motion picture film, or 120 or 620 rollfilm. The former gives negatives about $1x1\frac{1}{2}$ inches, 20 or 36 to a roll. The latter makes 12 pictures $2\frac{1}{4}x2\frac{1}{4}$ inches (some take 8 or 16 shots on a roll.) The fastest films are available in both these sizes.

All things being equal, you can make somewhat larger, sharper enlargements from the larger negative, but this should not be a deciding factor, since it is possible to make superb 11x14 prints from, say, half of a 35-mm negative.

The fastest lenses are available only on 35-mm cameras. This is due to the fact that making an $f/2$ lens, for instance, for a 120 rollfilm camera would be optically impractical and prodigiously expensive.

Two More Typical Available-Light Cameras.

(A)   SINGLE-LENS REFLEX, 120 ROLL FILM. The subject is viewed through the taking lens until the instant of exposure, they usually have a focal-plane shutter with a wide range of speeds, interchangeable lenses, and adaptability to extreme close-ups. This is the Reflex 66 (Courtesy Sterling-Howard Corp.).

(B)   BOX-TYPE CAMERAS. Low in price, generally non-adjustable, though some have a choice of two or three apertures. Some models feature reflex-type view for bright image of subject. This is the Brownie Reflex 20 (Courtesy Eastman Kodak Co.).

Therefore, rollfilm models have maximum apertures of $f/2.8$ at best; most have $f/3.5$. Lenses on 35-mm instruments of top quality generally open to $f/2$, $f/1.8$, $f/1.5$, or $f/1.4$. More modestly priced ones may have $f/2.8$ or $f/3.5$.

Concerning film size, another factor is economy. In available-light work especially, it is important to be generous with film. You will be dealing with situations that literally can never be recaptured (as "arranged" and studio-lighted setups can). You must be prepared to protect yourself from wrong guessing at exposures in tricky light situations, by shooting perhaps three frames for each picture you expect to get. (This procedure is called *bracketing* exposures— making an extra shot with more exposure and one with less, so that one negative will certainly be usable.)

By far the cheapest way to buy film is in bulk rolls of 35-mm, which brings the cost down to a fraction of a cent a shot. And 120 rollfilm, no matter how cheaply you buy it, will cost about three cents per negative. However, film cost, when it is so low, should not be a primary influencing factor in choosing a camera.

If you decide on economical 35-mm, remember that you must pay for this economy by the painstaking technique necessary to get clean, scratch-free pictures from 35-mm film. You may waste so much paper in the process of getting a fine print that it will outweigh the difference in film cost.

Which One Is Best For YOU?

Here is one consideration you must not overlook: with which type of camera do *you prefer* to work? Which feels best in your hands? Your camera store will let you handle them, sometimes rent them, or take them out on approval before purchase. If you can get one on this basis, and shoot a few rolls of film with it, your effort will be repaid.

Among rollfilm models there are three broad types: the folding cameras (like the Ikontas), the single-lens reflexes (like the Hasselblad), and the twin-lens reflexes (like the Rolleiflex).

BOX CAMERA, AVAILABLE LIGHT. Two bank tellers and a clock make an interesting composition — but the important fact about this available-light picture is that it was made with an ordinary box camera. The fixed exposure was 1/45 second at f/11; Schwalberg developed the Tri-X film for 15 minutes in D-23, slightly longer than normal. To use a simple camera in a situation like this, try the "backward" reading of the exposure meter, described on page 40.

Among 35-mm choices there are single-lens reflexes (like the Pentax), and the direct viewfinder-rangefinder types (such as the Leica and Nikon).

In almost every sub-category, there are cameras at high, medium, and low prices. You get just about what you pay for; buy the finest camera you can afford, but don't regret being unable to buy the finest one on the market.

A directory of photographic products, such as the one published annually by *Popular Photography*, can help you in making your choice. It has detailed descriptions of all cameras of every type, and photographs of most of them.

To assist you in shopping for an available-light camera, however, here is a list of a few of the most popular makes and models. Box and simple folding cameras have been eliminated, because the assumption is that if you are seriously interested in working with available light, you will want a camera with a fairly fast lens and some range of shutter speeds, as well as a focusing adjustment.

In each category, the "ideal" or most highly favored cameras are listed first, followed by others of fine quality. Prices are approximate manufacturers' list available at the time of this publication; check with your dealer for exact current prices.

Rollfilm Cameras

MAMIYA AUTO 6. 120 roll film, Zuiko $f/3.5$ lens, shutter 1 to 1/500 second, coupled rangefinder. $100.

REVERE EE-127. 127 roll film, Raptar $f/2.8$ lens, fully automatic exposure control, coupled rangefinder, built-in meter. $140.

35-mm Cameras

LEICA M-3. Summicron $f/2$ lens, shutter 1 to 1/1000 second, wide choice of interchangeable lenses. $399.

CONTAX II, IIIa. Sonnar $f/1.5$ lens, shutter 1 to 1/1250 second, wide choice of interchangeable lenses. IIa, $268. IIIa, with built-in exposure meter, $288.

NIKON S-3. SP. Nikkor $f/1.4$ lens, shutter 1 to 1/1000 second, wide choice of interchangeable lenses. $270 to $545.

CANON. Canon $f/1.8$ lens, shutter 1 to 1/1000 second, wide choice of interchangeable lenses. $250. VI-T, with built-in meter, $279-$420.

(The cameras listed above might be called the "Big Four" of 35-mm rangefinder photography. Every professional who uses 35-mm owns at least one of them. No amount of discussion will establish which is "best;" every photographer has his preference. A typical pro opinion: "The Nikon is the Cadillac of cameras; the Leica is the Rolls Royce." Another might compare the Contax with the Canon. The alphabetical listings that follow represent only a very few of the 35-mm cameras well suited to available-light work.)

AIRES V. Coral $f/1.9$ lens, shutter 1 to 1/400 second, $130.

ARGUS C44-R. Cintar $f/2.8$ lens, shutter 1/10 to 1/300 second. $100.

CERTO SUPER DOLLINA II. Tessar $f/2.8$ lens, shutter 1 to 1/500 second. $75.

KODAK RETINA IIIc. Xenon $f/2$ lens, shutter 1 to 1/500 second. $175.

KODAK SIGNET 50, 80. Ektanar $f/2.8$ lens, shutter ¼ to 1/250 second. $88-$130.

MINOLTA SUPER A. Rokkor $f/1.8$ lens, shutter 1 to 1/400 second. $150.

VOIGTLANDER PROMINENT. Nokton $f/1.5$ lens, shutter 1 to 1/500 second. $230-$280.

Single-Lens Reflex Cameras

(These cameras permit you to see your picture through the taking lens up to the instant of exposure. There are both 35-mm and roll-film models.)

ALPA 7. 35-mm Macro-Switar $f/1.8$ lens, shutter 1 to 1/1000 second, wide choice of interchangeable lenses. $499. (Other models at lower prices.)

BESELER B TOPCON. Topcon $f/1.8$ lens, shutter 1 to 1/1000 second. $295.

EXAKTA VX IIa. 35-mm. Xenon $f/1.9$ lens, shutter to 1/1000 second, automatic diaphragm which resets to desired stop after focusing. $370. Many other lenses available, bringing price as low as $280.

HASSELBLAD 500C. 120 roll film. Planar $f/2.8$ lens, shutter 1 to 1/500 second, back detachable for interchange of films.

HEILAND PENTAX H-3. Takumar $f/1.8$ lens, shutter 1 to 1/1000 second. $190.

PRAKTINA FX. 35mm. Tessar $f/2$ lens, shutter 1 to 1/1000 second. $150.

Twin-Lens Reflex Cameras

(There is only one leader in this category, but there are numerous other cameras with fine lenses and good mechanical construction which will deliver comparable results at much lower cost. Again, this is only a partial list. All these cameras use 120 roll film.)

ROLLEIFLEX AUTOMATIC. Xenotar $f/3.5$ lens, shutter 1 to 1/500 second, automatic shutter-cocking with film advance. $250. With $f/2.8$ Xenotar lens, $300.

MAMIYAFLEX C2. Interchangeable lenses, standard Sekor $f/2.8$. Shutter 1 to 1/400 second. $170.

MINOLTA AUTOCORD. Rokkor $f/3.5$ lens, shutter 1 to 1/500 second, automatic shutter cocking. $100.

ROLLEICORD Va. Xenar $f/3.5$ lens, shutter 1 to 1/500 second. $100.

RICOHMATIC 225. Rikenon $f/3.5$ lens, shutter 1 to 1/500 second. $100.

YASHICAMAT LM. Yashinon $f/3.5$ lens, shutter 1 to 1/500 second, built-in light meter. $80.

Sub-Miniature Cameras

(These instruments use film smaller than 35-mm, usually 16-mm movie film. This increases the difficulty of achieving good quality prints of acceptable size, but they offer the advantage of very small size.)

GAMI 16. Esamitar $f/1.9$ lens, shutter $\frac{1}{2}$ to 1/1000 second. $298.

MINICORD III. Heligor $f/2$ lens, shutter 1/10 to 1/400 second. $140.

MINOX III S, B. Special cartridge film, 50 exposures. Lens $f/3.5$, shutter $\frac{1}{2}$ to 1/1000 second. $140. With built-in light meter, $170.

MAMIYA SUPER-16. Lens $f/3.5$, shutter $\frac{1}{2}$ to 1/200 second. $40.

MINOLTA-16. Lens $f/2.8$, shutter 1/30 to 1/500 second. $40.

This listing has omitted press-type and other cameras which are, of course, adaptable to available-light photography but not ideally suited to it.

Are There "Extras" To Buy?

All you really need for any kind of photography is a camera. But there are some accessories that make shooting easier and results more uniformly good. As far as available-light technique is concerned, let's just mention the possibility of acquiring an extra lens or two (if your camera accepts interchangeable lenses), a lens hood, and an exposure meter.

The Long And Short Of Lenses

Some cameras, mostly rollfilm single-lens reflexes and all types of 35-mm, permit you to use lenses of longer or shorter focal length than the "normal" lens furnished with the camera. Long-focus lenses bring distant objects closer; short-focus lenses have a wider angle of view. The advantages of both in available-light work are apparent.

If you can shoot a candid portrait from 15 feet away, instead of approaching to within 5 feet, you can remain unobtrusive, perhaps completely unnoticed in a crowd. The long-focus lens also enables you to shoot successfully when you must keep at a distance from the subject: at a sports event, at a meeting, in a theatre. In addition, long-focus lenses (sometimes incorrectly called telephotos, although at times they are true telephotos) produce less distortion of the image than you would get in a close-up with a normal lens.

The advantage of a wide-angle lens will be immediately apparent when you find yourself shooting in a small room, or otherwise cramped for space. In all those situations where you would like to take about three paces backward to get everything you want in the picture, but find there's a wall in the way, the wide-angle lens is the only answer. Since much available-light work is done indoors, these situations arise frequently.

If you own a simple box or folding camera, or a twin-lens reflex, you won't be able to use interchangeable lenses, but you should try to acquire a set of supplementary close-up lenses for portraiture and detail work, such as a shot of hands at work, or a piece of machinery.

A lens hood is a kind of "poor relation" among camera accessories. It doesn't cost much, but it's an inconvenience. Perhaps you've thought of it as just one more gadget to handle — or perhaps you haven't thought of it at all. In ordinary photography, the shade can prevent extraneous light from striking the lens and causing flare on the negative. When you are working with available light, especially one kind of it, a shade is a virtual necessity. When the light is coming from one or more strong sources, and is not diffused or indirect, it is likely to strike your lens at some time as you move about from one shooting position to another. A lens hood — plus a little thought about your camera angle — can generally prevent the kind of disaster that comes from light-struck film. It's well worth its cost, and well worth the little inconvenience of using it.

Do You Need a Meter?

Every consistently successful photographer either uses an exposure meter or depends on his own long experience and careful judgment when it comes to determining exposures. And when it comes to available light, even an old hand at exposure-guessing can be fooled or confused. The best solution: get a meter.

Exposure Meters.

(A) REFLECTED-LIGHT EXPOSURE METERS are designed to measure the light reflected from the subject to the camera. Shown is the Weston Master IV (Courtesy Daystrom, Inc., Weston Instrument Div.).

(B) INCIDENT-LIGHT EXPOSURE METERS measure the light falling on the subject. (Either incident-light or reflected-light exposure meters are acceptable; the choice depends on your preference). The incident-light Norwood Super Director (Courtesy U. S. Photo Supply Co., Inc.).

(C) FOR POOREST LIGHT: Some new meters are designed to measure incredibly low light levels — even moonlight. This one is the Gossen Lunasix (courtesy Kling Photo Corp.).

(D) YOU NEEDN'T PAY A LOT for a good photoelectric exposure meter. Some models cost about $8. This reflected-light model is the Sekonic Auto-Lumi (Courtesy Sekonic, Inc.).

Let's consider only photoelectric meters, for two reasons: (1) the visual-extinction or "squint-through" type, at best, is not accurate enough and does not permit working in weak light; and (2) photoelectric meters are inexpensive enough nowadays (beginning at about $7.00) so that anyone can afford one. The one requirement in any meter is sensitivity to low-intensity light.

There are two ways of reading light intensity: by measuring the amount of light reflected from the subject toward the camera, and by measuring the amount of light falling on the subject from the light source. Both are perfectly dependable, and both methods have their partisans. Many meters permit measuring the light either way. Try both ways, decide on one, and stick to it. You will learn how to use a meter for available light in the next chapter.

What Film Should You Choose?

It seems simple enough: since the problem is inadequate light, choose the fastest film. That's a good beginning, but there are other things to think about: grain, contrast, and the kind of development you will use.

To begin with, let's ignore one kind of film: the extremely fine-grain products (like Kodak Panatomic-X and Adox KB 14) which sacrifice all speed for the sake of grainlessness. (High speed and fine grain, at their absolutes, are irreconcilable. You can't have both *completely*. But you can go a long way in both directions at the same time.)

This leaves us with three types of film for available light, which might be described as medium-speed, high-speed, and very high-speed. Here are some representative ones of each type:

TYPE 1 — Medium-speed
Plus-X, Verichrome Pan, Ilford FP-3, Isopan ISS, (ASA 64 to 160)
TYPE 2 — High-speed
Tri-X, Ilford HP-3 (ASA 200 to 400)
TYPE 3 — Very high-speed
Super Hypan, Ilford HP-S, Isopan Record (ASA 400 to 640)

(The ASA numbers given for each type refer to indexes established by the American Standards Association to provide a basis for comparison of film speeds.)

D. M. Ninzer

PIONEERING A NEW FILM. This shot of a boy in his bath was part of an experimental series made with Tri-X film before its release to the public. Light came from a shaded 60-watt bulb about five feet away, and exposure with a Contax was 1/25 second, f/2. The film was developed normally. In spite of the contrasty light source, the film's ability to resist shadow blocking-up is well demonstrated.

Pat Caulfield

RESTAURANT CANDID. Plus-X film was used for this shot, taken at San Francisco's Top of the Mark cafe. Since there are windows on all sides, even on overcast days it is possible to make good pictures without fast lenses and with very slow shutter speeds. This picture was made at 1/50 second, f/4.5, with a Rolleiflex. The light from the closest window gave modeling to the face, and light from across the room illuminated the shadow side.

You can see that each type of film is about twice as fast as the one before it. These ratings are all conservative, and represent manufacturers' recommendations for best results. In actual practice, however, workers with available light employ the films at ratings very much higher. Plus-X, for instance, is commonly exposed at ASA 200 to 320, while Tri-X is used at ASA 400, 650, 800, and even higher.

What Is "Normal" Film Speed?

What makes possible these fantastic departures from "recommended" speeds? Two things. First, in available-light work we do not fear underexposure as much as overexposure (see *Chapter 9*), so we are not so interested in "playing it safe." Second, today's films have much more latitude (acceptance of widely varying exposure without loss of quality) than manufacturers care to admit, so that proper use of vigorous high-speed developers easily permits doubling or tripling the basic rating.

If you associate with other photographers, you will receive a good deal of advice about your choice of film and every facet of the trade. If you are not careful, you will find yourself taking all this advice, and never shooting two consecutive rolls of the same film in the same way with the same processing.

Listen to all the experts, but make your own decision. Settle on one material and one way of working with it. If you find, after a fair trial, that you are not getting the results you wanted, consider changing. But don't be an emulsion grasshopper. Make it Plus-X and D-76 at ASA 200, or HP-3 and Acufine at ASA 800, or whatever you choose. But make your choice intelligently, and be loyal to it.

In summary: medium-speed films (except for Plus-X in 35-mm size) will be useful only when light is fairly good, and when finer grain is required. High-speed films are best for most available-light work (in the office, at the party, in the children's room). Very high-speed materials may be adapted to general purpose use, but find their real place when the light is truly miserable. With skilful processing, there need be no significant increase in grain.

Should You Develop Film Yourself?

The answer is emphatically *yes*, if you possibly can. To take advantage of heightened film speeds, you need careful and specialized developing, and unless you live in a large city you may not be able to get that at any price. Professional film processors, no matter how experienced, may have neither sympathy for nor interest in processing available-light work.

But the real reasons are that the procedure for developing film is so *easy*, and so satisfying! If you have visions of seesawing films through a row of messy trays, and pasting black paper across all the kitchen windows — forget them. All the "facilities" you need for expert film developing are these: a tank (that may cost as little as three dollars), a light-tight closet in which to load the tank (a two-minute job), and a kitchen sink (no need to black out the room). You will need buy only two or three chemicals; there is nothing to mix, nothing even to stain your fingers.

Start It Simply

Basic manuals of photography have detailed, illustrated instructions for the "mechanics" of processing, but here is all there really is to it:

Practice loading the tank a few times with a dummy roll of film (often supplied with it). When you can do it quickly and without a hitch, with your eyes closed, you're ready for the real thing. Step into the closet, load the film, close the tank, and step out. You're through with the "darkroom" work!

In the kitchen, pour developer into the tank. Let the developer remain for the prescribed time, usually 12 to 16 minutes, agitating it slightly every few minutes. If room temperature varies much from 68°, place the tank in a bath of warm or cool water, and use a tank thermometer to check it. When the time is up, pour the solution back into its bottle, and pour in a stop bath for a minute. Pour this out, and follow with a fixing bath — five minutes if you use a rapid fixer.

Pour the fixer back in its bottle, take the lid off the tank, and leave the film (still on the reel in the tank) under running water for an hour. Then remove the film from the reel, hang it with a film clip in a dust-free, out-of-the-way place, and sponge off the excess water carefully. Then admire your handiwork! There's nothing in photography quite so gratifying.

Now that we have made developing sound so attractively simple, let's make one big reservation. There is a lot to know about processing besides its mechanics, and a lot to remember. Some of this you will find in *Chapter 8*. Some you will learn only through experience.

When it comes to printing, of course, you will need some kind of working darkroom, and you will have to make more of an investment in equipment and supplies. But if you are serious about available-light photography, you will reach a point where you will not want to trust your beautiful negatives to anyone but yourself.

Pat Caulfield

AGAINST THE LIGHT. A window or other light source, in which all detail will block up at normal exposure, can make a good background, as it does for this tray of fish heads in a market. Aperture, shutter speed and focus combined to give this result: exposure, based on weak electric light overhead, was 1/10 second at f/3.5; the wide aperture also helped to limit depth of field and keep other parts of the picture from distracting.

CHAPTER 3

THE BASICS OF PHOTOGRAPHY
- - - and How They Work Together in Available-Light Technique

The Three Fundamental Camera Functions

Three factors contribute to the making of a photographic image:

Aperture

Shutter speed

Focus

On all but the simplest cameras, these factors are indicated by variable settings. (On box-type cameras the same factors are present, but their settings have been predetermined for you.)

APERTURE, the opening of the iris diaphragm of the lens, determines the *amount of light* from the subject which will be permitted to reach the film.

SHUTTER SPEED determines the *length of time* during which a given amount of light is allowed to reach the film.

FOCUS refers to the point at which an image of the subject is brought into *sharpness* on the film plane. It is controlled by adjusting the lens-to-film distance, in proportion to varying lens-to-subject distances.

These three factors are interrelated. Each influences the others directly or indirectly. When the aperture is small, the shutter speed must be relatively slow. When a fast shutter speed is required, a wider aperture must be used. When a wider aperture is used, the focusing must be more precise.

Depth Of Field

Aperture has a second important function, besides controlling the amount of light passing through the lens. It determines *depth of field* — the zone within which parts of a subject will be sharp. At $f/22$, which is often the smallest aperture setting on a rollfilm or miniature camera, everything in the picture might be sharp from a few feet away to infinity, with the focus set for, say, 20 feet. (This depends on the *focal length*, or lens-to-film distance, of the particular camera.)

At the other extreme, with an aperture of $f/3.5$ or $f/2$, the depth of field might be only a foot or two, so that focusing would become a matter of great precision.

With 35-mm cameras, usually having lenses with a focal length of 50 mm (about two inches), depth of field is much less restricted at any given aperture than with larger cameras and longer focal-length lenses. For example, a 50-mm lens at $f/3.5$, focused at 10 feet, has a depth of field of 4 feet 5 inches, while a 75-mm lens (typical of 120 rollfilm cameras), at the same aperture and focus setting, has only a 2 foot 10 inch depth of field.

Using The Three Factors In Available Light

Remember that available-light technique is not only a way of dealing with reduced light; it is a whole *system* of photography. It involves new ways of looking at subject matter, new ways of interpreting mood and movement.

Aperture, shutter speed, and focus are all parts of this system, as they must be for any kind of picture-taking. But in available-light work they have a special kind of importance.

The Wide-Open "Eye" . . .

Apertures, generally speaking, should be as wide as possible. Professionals who use available-light technique most often work with a stop of $f/5.6$ or wider. Many own $f/1.5$ lenses and shoot almost everything "wide open," adjusting for various light conditions by changing shutter speed. Of course, as some pictures in this book demonstrate, you don't need expensive top-speed lenses for available-light shooting today. Nevertheless, the wider the aperture, the better — and with wider aperture you can handle more difficult situations.

THE WIDE-OPEN EYE. Catching action near its peak, Wolfe was able to shoot at 1/25 second, f/1.5, with a Contax, on Plus-X. Notice that, even at such a wide aperture, there is a lot of depth of field when the subject is not too close to the camera. Although the circus has its own spotlights and floods, they are for circus purposes, not for photography; so the big show is really an available-light situation. This shot was taken from a balcony as the trapeze artist swung upside down.

"REAL-LIFE" FAMILY PICTURES. Focus was centered on the father's face, and at the wide aperture of f/2 the other faces are a bit out of focus, but not enough to detract from the picture's success. When the camera has gained everyone's confidence, as it has here, family group photographs are really spontaneous and full of life. This shot was made at 1/25 second, with a Contax and Plus-X film, which was developed, Wolfe says, "by an old West Coast technique: 11 minutes in Microdol and 4 minutes in D-76."

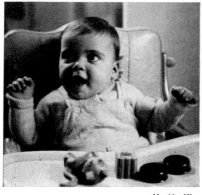

WAITING FOR LUNCH. This shot was made at 1/25 second, f/4; a Contax was used with Tri-X film rated at ASA 400. The baby is waiting for lunch in a kitchen which would actually be a good portrait studio; it has big windows facing east and west, one serving as main light and the other as fill-in, depending on the hour of the day.

. . . And The Slow "Wink"

Correspondingly, shutter speeds will ideally be slower. Beginners' manuals tell you that when the shutter is set as slow as 1/25 second, you must practice holding the camera steady or brace it on a solid support to avoid fuzzy results. This is true, but if you are going to work seriously in available-light situations, you will have to learn to take steady shots not only at 1/25, but at 1/10 and even 1/5. There is a professional working today who is known for his consistent ability to shoot at ½ second without support, and get sharp pictures; but that is a little too much to expect from most people, except for an occasional lucky shot.

Focus: The Easier The Better

Focusing is done either with an optical rangefinder or with a reflected groundglass image. Either way, it is easiest if the subject is well lighted. In available light, it usually isn't — so sharp focusing immediately becomes a problem. It is complicated too, in a way already suggested above: at wide apertures, with depth of field restricted, focusing *must* be precise. This is one of photography's typical frustrations: just when you need sharpness most, it's hardest to get.

The problem varies somewhat with the different types of camera. If yours has an optical rangefinder, all you can hope is that it is of good quality, with an image-registering system that is easy to see. It may be either of the split-image or the superimposed-image type. The latter is generally considered to be brighter and on the whole more satisfactory for available light.

The difficulty is somewhat less if you are using a single-lens reflex, such as the Exakta or the Alpa, because you will be working mostly with the widest aperture, and the groundglass image will be at its brightest. When you do shoot at less than maximum aperture, it is a great advantage to have an automatic or preset diaphragm which enables you to focus wide open and shoot at any aperture you like, without changing the setting.

In the case of a twin-lens reflex, you can improve matters by installing a "field lens" just beneath the groundglass; it brightens the

31

image considerably and in poor light it can mean the difference between a satisfactory reflection and none at all. This accessory costs about five dollars, and is well worth it. It will also be worthwhile to practice using the flip-up magnifier that is built into the hood on most twin-lens reflexes. The magnifier has the effect of increasing brightness as well as size.

In Practice: Some Examples

Let us suppose you want to photograph two children eating at a table, in a fairly well-lighted kitchen. You are using a 120 rollfilm camera with a 75-mm $f/3.5$ lens, and a Type 2 film like HP-3, at ASA 200. An exposure meter reading gives you these choices:

$$1/50 \text{ at } f/3.5$$
$$1/25 \text{ at } f/5.6$$
$$1/10 \text{ at } f/8$$
$$1/5 \text{ at } f/11$$

There are other factors to consider:

1. The children are about three feet apart — to get them both in the picture at short range you must shoot from one end of the table, putting one child much closer to the camera than the other.

2. There is a good deal of activity involved.

Your choice of exposure is influenced in one direction, then, by the desire to stop as much motion as possible, and in the other direction by the necessity of getting both children sharp in the picture.

This is where the element of focus enters. Your camera probably has a *depth of field scale*, either engraved on a plate at the back or directly opposite the focusing scale on the knob or on the lens. (If it does not, you should obtain a copy of such a scale — be sure that this scale matches your lens.) Learn to read this scale at a glance. It tells you the distance from the nearest to the farthest part of the subject that will be sharp at a given $f/$stop and focus setting.

Checking the scale for this situation, you would find that at 7 feet, and $f/3.5$, the depth of field is only 16½ inches. At $f/5.6$ it is 27 inches, still not quite enough to insure getting both children sharp. So you will use $f/8$, which gives you a 40-inch depth, and you will shoot at 1/10 second, holding the camera as steady as you can and

William Noyes & Pedro Guerrero

THEY WORK AT NIGHT. At night there are often areas of bright light which makes picture-taking quite easy. Exposure meter readings should always be made within the area of the activity, so the meter is not "deceived" by the large areas of darkness. Here, Noyes and Guerrero chose to use a slow shutter, 1/2 second, in order to stop down to f/5.6 for some depth of field. Their camera was a Rolleiflex and their film Tri-X.

Harry S. Lapow, from Popular Photography Picture Contest

watching for peaks of action when the slow shutter will catch the least blur. If you could back away to 9 feet, sacrificing the close-up quality, you would easily be able to shoot at 1/25, f/5.6.

If you were working in the same situation with a 35-mm camera and its 50-mm lens, you would have no trouble at all in exposing at 1/50 second, f/3.5, and you might even advance to 1/100, f/2.8, if the lens were that fast.

Let's Go To a Party!

By way of another example, let's move to a party with only normal incandescent room light. You want to get two kinds of pictures: overall shots that include many people and give a feeling of the party; and informal portraits of some of the guests. Let's say, to make it a bit easier, that you have a 35-mm camera with an f/2 lens, and that you will be loaded with a Type 2 film such as Tri-X, shooting at a high (though not emergency) rating of ASA 400.

A party is a difficult place in which to determine correct exposure. How will you use your meter? You might stand back as far as possible and point the meter at the whole gathering. You might walk around and take readings from the cheeks of selected individuals, incidentally making yourself more than a little conspicuous.

Probably the most useful reading in this case would be from the palm of your own hand, held at about waist level and turned to catch as much light as there is. (The waist-level reading would afford a fair compromise between sitting and standing guests.) You might repeat this reading at two or three different spots in the room, in case the lighting is deceptively uneven.

POIGNANCY VERSUS SHARPNESS. At a party, and working "from the hip" at a predetermined exposure made necessary by light conditions, a photographer is not always able to use a shutter speed ideal for the subject. In this case, Lapow's 35-mm Canon was set at 1/8 second, f/1.8. Spotting the transient expression on the little girl's face, he made the shot knowing the slow speed would not stop all motion. But his lens was at maximum aperture, and a faster shutter would have meant serious underexposure.

The best you can do in such an exposure situation will not be quite enough to produce ideal negatives. There are bound to be burned-out areas near lamps and abysmal shadows where heads are turned the wrong way. But this is, in a sense, what the eye sees in an overall glance at a roomful of people, as it takes some *visual* adjustment to perceive detail in highlights and shadows. You will have to be prepared to make such adjustment in *printing* your party pictures.

At any rate, a reading at a party might give these choices:

$$1/50 \text{ at } f/2$$
$$1/25 \text{ at } f/2.8$$
$$1/10 \text{ at } f/4$$
$$1/5 \text{ at } f/5.6$$

Unless you are interested only in a few people fairly closely grouped at almost equal distances from you, you will not be able to use the fastest shutter speed. But 1/25 second becomes quite possible, when you note from the depth of field scale that if you are focused at 10 feet, everything from about 7 to 20 feet will be sharp at $f/2.8$. Still, for large groups you may want to stop down farther. An aperture of $f/4$ with the short focal-length lens will guarantee sharpness from 6 feet to almost infinity, when you are focused at 12 feet!

The casual portraits are a different story. They are easier, because a good exposure based on flesh tones will produce a uniform negative that is not hard to print well. They are harder, though, because working at close range increases the necessity for precise focusing, and because you must watch for something that is most elusive — a revealing and communicative human expression.

Don't try to pick a spot in the room and maneuver your "victims" into it one after another. This simply puts another barrier between the subject and the film, and there are enough barriers already. He should be aware that there is a camera in the room, yes, and even that it is sometimes aimed at him. But he should not have the feeling that he is being inconvenienced or upset by the camera's presence.

Instead, survey the room (in advance, if possible) to find spots where the light is not only brightest but most diffused. (This is not necessarily a contradiction.) Give preference to indirect lamps that bounce light to the ceiling and shed a soft glow about their shades. Take meter readings at two or three feet from such light sources, from somebody's face, or your hand — "something you always have with you." During the course of the party, you will find that sooner or later everyone will be in a spot where you have taken readings.

It might be a good idea to allow a half-stop or so when the air is thick with smoke; but as far as quality is concerned, when smoke is diffused and floating high, it sometimes diffuses the light and makes conditions more favorable!

A typical exposure indication in such a place, if walls and ceiling are white or bright-colored, might be $1/100$ second at $f/2$. There is no reason not to shoot wide open and take advantage of the extra speed that will help you catch fleeting expressions, if you take extra care in focusing. Shooting from three feet, which is about as close as you will want to approach, you will have less than one foot of depth of field, but this will suffice if your focusing eye is sharp.

THE STREET AT NIGHT. After-dark wandering yields good pictures, like this silhouette of electricans working at an excavation in a Manhattan pavement. The cloud of steam diffuses some of the light from the bright bare bulbs, and prevents halation. The camera was a Rolleiflex, hand-held at 1/10 second with aperture of f/3.5. The Super-XX film was developed normally. Extreme contrast is not undesirable in such a silhouette.

CHAPTER 4

HOW "POOR" IS POOR LIGHT ?

- - - The Three Classes of Available-Light Situations

Available-light situations are of three main kinds:

1. Those in which the light is just slightly inadequate for good results with ordinary technique.

2. Those in which the light is definitely at a low level, but still sufficient for most work or recreation.

3. Those in which the light is truly abysmal, and presents a great challenge to the photographer.

For convenience, we will put each kind in a *Class* by itself. There is nothing rigid about these classifications; they are set up only as a reference aid to specific situations discussed later in this book. Here are some examples of the three classes.

CLASS I

Outdoors under a heavily clouded sky.

Indoors by a window with good daylight.

In deep shade, or on a screened porch.

CLASS II

In a well-lighted office, store, or factory.

In a playroom, nursery, or game room.

At a party or meeting.

CLASS III

In a tunnel or subway.

In a theater: audience or backstage.

Under streetlamp or storefront illumination.

These classifications are based on the *amount* of light in a situation. But the *quality* of the light is equally important. One of the most difficult photographic situations, for instance, is one in which there is a single strong source of light(a bare bulb, perhaps, or a direct floor lamp). This produces negatives of sufficient density but with excessive *contrast*, so that detail is lacking in both highlights and shadows, and the picture consists of areas of jet black and blank white. Ways of compensating for undesirable light quality are discussed in *Chapter 8*, and tips on avoiding excessive contrast are scattered throughout the paragraphs on particular situations.

Some Class 1 Situations

A Screened Porch

Here is a common situation, and one that lends itself well to picture-taking. If the porch is exposed to reflected daylight, is not too heavily shaded by trees and bushes, and is painted in a light color, you can make good photographs there with any box camera, using the fastest film at its maximum "normal" rating, around ASA 800.

Reading a Meter "Backward"

Here's how to tell whether there is enough light to make pictures with a camera having fixed aperture and shutter speed, by using an exposure meter "backward."

Most box cameras are set to operate at approximately 1/30 second, $f/11$. Set the exposure meter dial for the speed rating of ASA 800, then set 1/30 second opposite the $f/11$ mark. The meter will then indicate what the light level must be to get a proper exposure.

Hold the meter up to a face, or the palm of your hand, and see whether the needle swings far enough to indicate the necessary amount of light. If it does, you are ready to shoot. If it doesn't, try moving to a brighter corner of the porch, or wait until there is more light in the sky outside.

If you have a better camera, with a lens of $f/4.5$ or faster, you will be free to work in a more normal manner: take a light-meter reading, then decide what shutter speed you will need, and, in turn, what aperture will be required for it.

H. M. Kinzer

A SCREENED PORCH. Here is a picture taken in bright open shade which might have been made with the simplest camera, though a Voigtlander Superb twin-lens reflex was actually used. In a corner of a screened porch, on a hazy day, the light was good and well distributed. Exposure was 1/25 second at f/8 — close to the fixed setting of a box camera. Film was Plus-X, rated at ASA 200, developed in D-76 normally. A light print was made in order to preserve the delicate range of flesh tones.

41

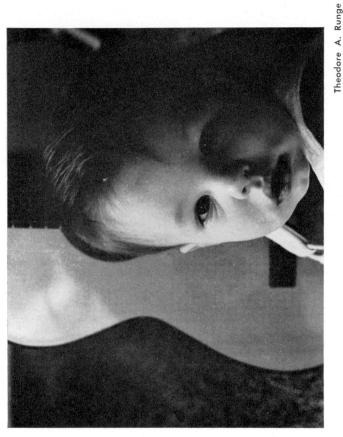

Theodore A. Runge

WINDOW LIGHT—INDIRECT. Proud father Runge propped his small son up in front of a guitar (which he manipulates as well as a camera). Outside there was a bright overcast sky. Rating Plus-X film at 160, he calculated an exposure of 1/30 second at f/5.6; normal development was for 3½ minutes in X-44.

42

Eliminate The Undesirable

On most porches, there will be a great deal of unwanted background detail: screen framework, swings, chairs, light fixtures. Thus, you will often choose the widest possible aperture, to reduce depth of field. At the same time, use a little ingenuity in taking a camera position which eliminates as much clutter as possible from the background.

One way to solve this background problem is to shoot outward, through the screen, toward the sky. In this way you may outline the subject against the sky. Remember though that it is the light *inside* the porch that concerns you. When you take a meter reading, be sure you are not taking in outdoor light too; hold the meter close to the subject. Always expose for the subject, and let the background go light or dark as it will.

Bright Window Light

Every house has a bright window corner, a family gathering place for reading, sewing, playing. It's a natural spot for wonderful pictures the year round, and when the light is especially good, with the sun coming directly through the window, you can get fine pictures there with the simplest cameras.

If you have a box or nonadjustable camera, follow the same "backward" exposure meter procedure as suggested for the screened porch. Since light is coming strongly from one direction only, you will have to be careful to take your readings at the same point where your subject will be — if not from the subject. A foot or two further into the room the light will fall off drastically.

With an adjustable camera, and at least a fairly fast lens, you can take much more liberty in choosing exposure. You can stop down the lens to include interesting objects in foreground and background: a lamp, needlework in a woman's lap, children's toys. You can use a faster shutter speed when there is motion, as with children at play.

Some Class II Situations

Wherever You Work . . .

If you work for a living, you spend at least a third of your life in the office, the store, the factory, or the shop. There is an opportunity for fine pictures where you work, interpreting your job and place of employment for people who do not know them, portraying the people who work with you as they really are, with sleeves rolled up and hands busy.

Most modern work situations are well lighted. This is all to the photographer's advantage; nearly every office, store, and factory can be called a Class II situation for our purposes — meaning that with modest equipment you can make satisfactory pictures there, and with a really good camera you can stop some motion and get a lot of depth of field under normal room lighting.

Take Meter Readings In Advance

Since it is a place where you spend a lot of time, and in which the light conditions are quite constant, you should take a number of exposure meter readings in advance, from various angles and at different spots. Use these readings as a guide to the limits within which you will be able to shoot — whenever you wish, without bothering to take new readings each time.

Most places of work take advantage of as much daylight as they can, and supplement it with artificial light, with increasing preference for fluorescent fixtures. In photography, the use of fluorescent lighting is a definite advantage over incandescent illumination. Ordinary light bulbs, even when some effort is made to diffuse their light, give a definite pattern of light and dark areas in a large work space. Fluorescents are, in effect, more like daylight, spreading an even level of light over the entire area. This means that you can move freely from areas near windows to spots that receive almost no daylight, without making very much change in exposure. Checking with the meter will tell you all you need to know about this in your particular situation.

Of course, sandhogs, subway motormen, and night workers will be in photo situations that are by no means so easy. If you want to make pictures of these, you will find some helpful ideas in the paragraphs on Class III situations.

If you work in a supervisory capacity, don't overlook the possibilities of available-light photography in supplementing time-and-motion study. A camera record of a store or office operation can be a

Pat Caulfield

MOMENT IN A FISH MARKET. In the confusion of a big New York City retail market, the photographer singled out a fish peddler and her counter, using a twin-lens reflex at its maximum aperture of f/3.5, and a shutter speed of 1/25 second. Lighting in the market was mixed tungsten and fluorescent, making the use of an exposure meter especially desirable. The film was Plus-X, developed in Promicrol for 14 minutes.

AVOIDING HIGHLIGHT WASHOUT. One common available-light
fault is overexposure, which drops all detail out of highlights.
Pierce has skilfully avoided it in this theater-rehearsal shot,
made on Agfa Isopan Record in a Nikon, with a wide-angle
25-mm Nikkor lens. His exposure was 1/15 second at f/4, and
he developed the film in UFG.

valuable aid in deciding on changes in procedures. There is a whole "career" here for the unobtrusive camera which so far has only been used at a fraction of its potential.

As For Parties . . .

A detailed plan for party shooting is embodied as an example in *Chapter 3, The Basics of Photography.*

. . . And Portraiture . . . And Kids.

You will find full coverage of these popular available-light subjects and situations in a later chapter.

Some Class III Situations

In The Theater

Nowadays, with the theater spreading outward from the centers of Broadway and its road-company tours, there are dramatic performances at some time during the year in almost every town in the country. Besides professional companies, there are community theaters, children's theaters, shows put on by clubs and organizations, and high-school and college theatricals.

Because of the requirements of stage lighting, theater situations are almost always difficult to photograph well. Not only is the light level generally low, but light comes mostly from strong single sources, with the footlights often acting as a rather inadequate fill-in illumination.

Shoot The Show

If you want to shoot during a performance or rehearsal, it will be a great help if you can arrange to go onstage at some time when the set is lighted as it will be for the show itself, and make some exposure meter readings. Move around the stage as much as you can, noting the low and high extremes of light intensity, so that you will be able to determine lens settings accurately as the actors move through their parts during the performance.

If you can't arrange to take meter readings from the stage itself, try to sit as close to the stage as possible, and take readings from all parts of the lighted area.

If your camera takes interchangeable lenses, and you own a long-focus lens, you will want to use it for stage photography, even if you are sitting rather close to the proscenium.

Go Backstage

There is a lot more to theater photography than simply recording what happens on the stage. In the case of amateur or community theatricals, you may not find it difficult to get permission to go backstage, into the corridors and dressing rooms, where the actors and dancers step out of character, out of costume and make-up. It's another world of its own, and fascinating to photograph. If you have a friend or acquaintance among the management, approach him from the publicity angle, and offer some prints from the pictures you hope to get.

Off-stage, you may find the lighting even more tricky and difficult than on-stage. In the corridors and behind the sets, the only light source is usually a bare bulb hanging from above, throwing a burning glare on foreheads and cheekbones and leaving eye-sockets and lower lips in blackest shadow. This means, of course, contrasty pictures, which you may be able to correct to some extent in processing. You can help by being sure not to *over*expose.

In the dressing rooms the light will also tend to be very contrasty, with strong lights overhead and around make-up mirrors, and little illumination elsewhere. But you will have good luck if you determine exposure by taking an advance reading from your hand held out toward the dressing-table lights, in about the position that an actor's face would occupy.

How To "Set Off" The Subject

It is crowded backstage, and you will be concerned with picking out one face or figure and isolating it from the turmoil as much as you can. For this, a wide aperture is your best friend. You can seldom hope to find an uncluttered background in such a place, even if you are able to "arrange" the situation to some extent. Even if lighting conditions did not demand it, you would want to shoot consistently at your widest aperture. The only exception would be if you were trying to show how many things go on in the small space at once — then of course you would stop down somewhat (use a smaller aperture).

Theatrical Portraits

Because actors and actresses are generally quite at ease before a camera, you can make fine portraits of them in their "natural

UNDER RAW STAGE LIGHTS. Three cast members of an off-Broadway production discuss their roles during a break. Pierce daringly permitted the light itself to appear in the picture; flare did not intrude on the image he wanted. With a Nikon and 25-mm Nikkor wide-angle lens, he exposed Isopan Record 1/15 second at f/4, and developed in UFG.

49

MOOD UNDERGROUND. A nearly deserted subway car, stopped at a station at night, has a forlorn look. This picture catches its moods, and the lone passenger seems lost in the train's emptiness. Shaman used a twin-len reflex and shot at 1/25 second, f/5.6, on Tri-X film.

habitat," portraits that look candid (because the subjects are not camera-conscious) but actually are not (because you have their cooperation). For portraits like this, you can moderate the harsh stage lighting by working near a white-painted wall or a light-colored part of the set. This will reflect some of the strong light into shadow areas and help reduce contrast.

In A Subway

One American in ten lives in a city that has a subway, and several millions more visit these cities each year, so subway photography is a fertile field — and a natural one for available-light technique. The trend is toward brightening up station platforms and trains, but the general light level remains pretty low.

In a well-lighted subway car, you will be able to shoot easily at $f/3.5$, at perhaps 1/10 second on fast film. On some platforms, however, you will have difficulty in getting good results at $f/2$ and 1/5 second.

In this book are some examples of very different kinds of pictures made in subways.

At Night On The Street

One photographer in search of a new project to challenge his imagination posed a model under a red-and-green traffic light in the dead of night, and made some black-and-white pictures of her, with no light whatever except the colored traffic lights. He wanted to see how much more sensitive his film was to red than to green. He found out — and in the process demonstrated that images could be recorded by instantaneous exposure with one of the most unpromising light sources imaginable.

Most of us won't have occasion to try anything like this, since it doesn't produce very good pictures — it only proves a point. But we might want to try making pictures by the kind of light that is to be found on city streets at night: streetlamps, theater marquees, store-fronts. Such pictures can be quite good, and there are some factors that help make this night shooting easy.

In front of a movie theater, for instance, you will often find a kind of floodlighting which makes it possible to use reasonably fast

THROUGH A WINDOW. Prowling the streets of New York at night, Aleshire spotted this subject in an Automat, and shot through a plate glass window with his Alpa 7 single-lens reflex. He decided on an exposure of 1/50 second at f/4 on Tri-X, and developed in Promicrol. During printing, extensive burning-in was necessary in the area of the woman's hand, to get even a little detail in the brilliant highlight.

shutter speeds. (This is actually a Class II situation, if the light is good enough.) You can also stand beside a lighted store window display, shooting candidly, bracing yourself and your camera against a solid wall for steadiness enough to use the very slow shutter speeds.

Don't overlook the possibilities in pattern shots made with very slow shutters, or time exposures, utilizing the light trails created by passing automobiles. Then there are the abstractions you can make by aiming at lights and flashing signs, and moving the camera with the shutter open. The potentialities here are unlimited, and with even the simplest camera you can use not only black-and-white but color film, regulating the time of exposure accordingly.

Richard Pousette-Dart, from Popular Photography Picture Contest

CHAPTER 5

PORTRAITS, CHILDREN, HOBBIES

- - - Available-Light Subjects and Techniques

Faces By Available Light

Portraiture is the biggest branch of photography. People's faces are more photographed than fashion models, dogs, cats, and manufactured goods combined. It's true that a good part of the total can be charged off to passport and license photos, high-school and college yearbook mug-shots, and studio pictures. But it is also a fact that some of photography's most outstanding contributions to our life and culture have been great portraits: Brady's *Lincoln*, Steichen's *J. P. Morgan*, Karsh's *Churchill*, W. Eugene Smith's *Schweitzer* — and dozens more.

Now, in a day when it is possible to make fine pictures without artificial light and without long exposures, more camera portraitists are working with available-light. The most skilful are able to penetrate deeper than the "arranged" features of a face, to catch something of the person inside, to *reveal*—which is the camera's greatest work.

PORTRAIT OF A CHILD. The photographer's small daughter Joanna and her cat Snowbell had their portrait made by comparatively weak daylight from a window. There is good detail and modeling on one side of the face (and the cat), and just enough on the other side to avoid a total blackout — an effect which Pousette-Dart preserved by careful printing. His camera was a Leica with Plus-X film; exposure 1/25 second at f/2.8.

Making portraits by available light, so far as technique is concerned, is deceptively easy. You place your subject (or find your subject) in a given situation, determine exposure, decide on angle and range, and shoot. But there is much more involved. Consider the *quality* of the light, as well as the quantity. Consider the *setting* — background, foreground, what should be left in the picture and what removed. And consider the *response* — the subject's relationship and reaction to the camera and to you.

In portraiture, more than in other available-light situations, you have some choice in these matters. (When it's a party, for instance, or a chess game, or kids in the playroom, you generally must take what you can get.) So by all means use this opportunity to create your own situation. Move the subject to a spot where the light is more ample and more pleasant, but where the subject can still feel at ease.

The most successful available-light portraits seem to be made either near windows, or under indirect artificial light, or a combination of the two. A window is probably the best of all light sources for a home portrait studio. If there is a corner with windows on both sides, so much the better.

Before You're Ready To Shoot

Place a model near the window and study the effect of the light. Note how much of the face is in shadow when the model turns a three-quarter profile toward the light. See how much change is made when the model turns very slightly. Remember that the shadow areas will be darker in a print than they seem to your eyes. Consider carefully whether some lack of detail will contribute to the result or detract from it. Prepare some kind of reflector, (cardboard, cloth, or metal foil) if you like, to lighten dark areas. Perhaps it will help to turn on the room light. Careful observation of what the light does can save a lot of disappointing experimentation.

WINDOW LIGHT FOR PORTRAITS. There's no place like a window for making available-light portraits. The light is flattering, soft and diffused. In this case Fried has placed young actress Susan Strasberg so that the wall at her right served as a reflector to pour some light back into the shadowed side of her face. This resulted in an admirable range of tones, avoiding the excessive blocking of shadows that too often come with one-sided lighting. Fried used a twin-lens reflex and Super-XX film; exposure 1/5 second at f/3.5.

Larry Fried, from Popular Photography Picture Contest

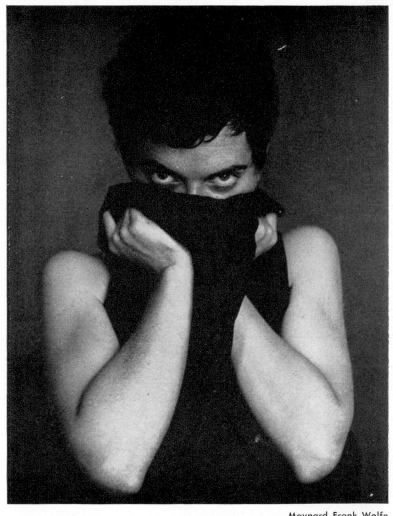

OFFBEAT PORTRAIT. Intimacy and spontaneity of expression are not difficult to get when the camera ceases to be a stranger to the subject. Wolfe made this intriguing picture under normal room light on Tri-X film in a Rolleiflex, at 1/25 second, f/4.

Let's look at what light does in a specific case. Suppose you have an overhead fluorescent fixture, bright enough to illuminate a small room well, and a small table lamp which you can move about. Again with the model's permission, see how the shadows fall on the face with only the overhead fixture turned on. Usually the light will be better distributed than if the lamp were a conventional incandescent bulb. Ask the model to move to one side of the room, not directly under the light. This further modifies and softens the light, but there will probably be shadows in the eyes, and under the nose and chin. Now turn on the table lamp, directing it so that its light is not on the face, but on a wall. Move your model once more into various positions, noting how the combination of two light sources affects highlights and shadows.

Naturally, when you are making portraits you will not go to all this trouble. So much maneuvering destroys spontaneity, which is the most valuable attribute of natural-light portraits. That is precisely why it is a good idea to run through these exercises in advance, as a kind of "homework," to familiarize yourself with light and what it does. Even if you have studied conventional portrait lighting with floodlights, you'd better rehearse with available light before you shoot. As you rehearse, it would be a good idea to take meter readings to familiarize yourself with the kind of exposures you may expect to use. Compare the readings of highlight and shadow areas, and consider using a compromise exposure; it will be necessary if you want to keep detail in all parts of the picture.

What Can You Do About the Setting —
The Background And Props?

If you can avoid it, don't do anything. A window frame and a plain curtain make a good background. Stay away from chintzy drapes, flower-patterned wallpaper, and tapestried upholstery. Use a simple straight chair if you like. Hands can hold a book, a pipe, or needlework, but such props should generally be played down in the picture. Interest can be added by showing the subject in relation to his occupation or hobby, but when this is overdone it becomes something other than a portrait.

What you seek most of all in a portrait is a *picture of a person, in depth*. This is more than a mirror-image of flesh and bone. It is a

A CONDUCTOR LISTENS. Charles Munch, leader of the Boston Symphony, was hearing a replay of a recording and scanning a score when Martin Dain got this revealing portrait. There was a window about ten feet away at the subject's right, and no other light in the room. Dain used a Leica with an f/1.5 lens, but stopped it down to f/5 and shot at 1/60 second.

reflection of personality, of individuality, through the expression on the face. You cannot coax such an expression out of your subject, and you cannot command it.

Available-light technique makes it easier for you to *draw* the personality to the surface. Working without paraphernalia, and handling the camera as though it were a participant, you encourage openness and honesty in your model.

Talk to the model as you shoot, and work with a shutter speed that can catch the expressions of speech. Establish a common ground; understand the model, and you can hardly fail at portraiture.

There are some fine examples of available-light portraiture in this book, made under a great variety of conditions. They are not here only for decoration; each one has something to teach you. Pay less attention to details of shutter speed and aperture than to the quality of light. Technical data are significant only for a particular situation, but what you learn about light quality is always valid.

Children At Play

Children will always be the most popular subject for amateur picture-taking. Probably well over a third of all amateur photographs are of children. Most of them are made in one of two ways: outdoors in sunlight, or indoors with flash or flood.

A great deal of a child's activity is centered indoors: in kitchen and bath, playroom and bedroom. But it's pretty hard to keep him unaware of the camera, and get those really natural, spontaneous, essence-of-childhood shots, if you have to string up floodlamps or bang away with flashbulbs.

Again, the answer is available-light technique. Many of the situations in which children find themselves are identical with those described under other headings, but there are some special problems. Here are some tips on a few representative situations.

Snap 'Em Splashing!

You don't ordinarily think of the bathtub as an ideal spot for photography — unless you happen to be a specialist in soapsudsy cheesecake. But for children it is perfect. Most of them love the water, and don't get enough of it at the beach or in the wading pool. The bath is a kind of a treat, except for the part about scrubbing the ears. It's a natural situation for exuberance and action; any busy mother will testify to that!

Most bathrooms are well lighted and have white or bright walls that help keep up the level of illumination. Take meter readings in advance, as you always do when you can. You will probably find it possible to shoot at $f/3.5$ or even $f/4.5$, using a rather slow shutter speed. With a faster lens, you can choose a faster shutter speed that will stop most of the motion. (These estimated exposures are based on readings in a typical small, bright bathroom with a 100-watt bulb in a diffusing fixture.)

If the room is small, and your camera has interchangeable lenses, use a wide-angle lens. It has the effect of letting you "step back" farther than the walls will permit.

Keep some lens tissue handy to protect your camera from the inevitable splashes.

The Playroom

Whether it's a corner of the bedroom or a well-appointed room by itself, the place where children play is a place to take a picture. It is one place where an adult must not be an intruder. If he comes in at all, it must be on the children's terms. Whether you enter as a participant in the play, or as a sympathetic and welcome observer, is a matter for you to decide. But it must be one way or the other, and the camera must be fully accepted too.

Play space is usually well lighted, often near a window, so this kind of shooting is quite average for Class II situations. Remember, though, that if the light is coming mainly or entirely from one direction (as from a window), the angle from which you shoot must be carefully considered. Otherwise faces will be heavily shadowed,

---

BY A TABLE LAMP. The simplest of indoor light sources was used for this child's portrait. The girl was looking almost into the light, and there was enough low-level illumination elsewhere in the room to catch detail in her hair. Duckworth used a Contax loaded with Ilford HP-3 film, and exposed at 1/10 second, f/4.

Paul Duckworth, from Popular Photography Picture Contest

PORTRAITS WITH A DIFFERENCE: Here are two informal portraits, made at different times and places, and with different kinds of cameras. The picture above was taken in an office, with a couple of photographs tacked to the wall, out of focus, adding to the interest. Light came from a window about 6 feet away, at left, and a small fluorescent desk lamp nearby at right. Exposure was 1/10 second at f/3.5, with a twin-lens reflex camera. The portrait below was made with normal room light only, and an abstract painting for background. The subject was talking casually while the photographer worked. He used a 35-mm camera, shooting at 1/25, f/15.

and toys and activity will be obscured by underexposure. It's a good idea to sit on the floor beneath or beside the window: thus when action turns toward you and the camera, it is also turned toward the light. The same is true for a lamp if there is one in the room.

People Enjoying Themselves

When you're with people having fun, and have a camera with you, you're set for shooting fun yourself. When it's in a game room, a home workshop, or any recreation area indoors, you will want to work with available light — for the same two big reasons: to avoid disturbing your subjects, and to preserve the natural atmosphere of the setting.

Shoot-It-Yourself

If you are a serious photographer, the current trend toward do-it-yourself hobbies is nothing new to you. Your friends who are learning to build coffee tables, kitchen shelves, and doghouses in their basements are finding out about the kind of satisfaction you felt when you developed your first roll of film. Their enthusiasm, their mistakes, and their triumphs are wonderful subject matter for your available-light camera.

A cellar workshop is not an ideal photo situation. Your handyman will have plenty of light over his lathe, jigsaw, and drillpress, but this situation is roughly comparable to what you'd find in a theatrical dressing room: strong light from one or two sources, generally overhead.

The do-it-yourselfer is interested in the piece he is working on. You want to include that, of course, and the hands that are doing the work. But you also want to include his face, to get some of that rapt concentration, frustration, or glow of accomplishment that flash across his visage as he works.

One professional, wanting some high-quality home workshop pictures without flash or flood, induced his woodworking friend to put a sheet of wrinkled aluminum foil under the bed of his lathe, on the pretext that he could see what he was doing more easily. You

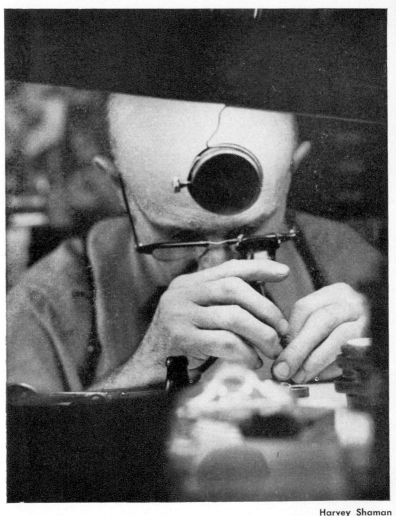

CLOSE WORK, HOT LIGHT. Craftsmen like this watchmaker work under bright light which covers just a small area. If you're lucky, some of the light spills and bounces off the workbench to lighten the shadows. Here the exposure was based on the hands, focal point of the picture, and other areas did not suffer much lack of detail. Shaman used a Rolleiflex, and light came from fluorescent tubes above the workman's hands.

probably won't be able to set up such a natural reflector without unduly disturbing the shop routine, but there's more than one way to get a good picture.

If you can shoot from the opposite side of the power tool, looking toward the worker and keeping direct light from your lens, by all means do it. Base your exposure on a reading from his hands and the work they are doing, and open one stop wider. This will usually provide a compromise negative, in which you can either hold back the face or burn in the hands to get a well-balanced print. Don't worry about getting detail in other areas. A workshop is typically so cluttered or so full of distracting elements that it will be an advantage to concentrate attention on a small area by underexposing the rest.

When the hobbyist is working by window light the problem is simpler, because the light is more evenly distributed in the work area — though it may be weaker on the whole.

More important than these technical details is the relationship you establish with your subject. He must feel that what you are doing is like what he is doing — enjoying yourself while overcoming obstacles imposed by the medium. In his case, a block of hardwood; in your case a strip of film with tremendous possibilities but very definite limitations.

This same approach is valid for every situation in which your camera attempts to capture some of the subject's enjoyment and fulfillment — any hobby, pastime, or diversion.

NIGHTCLUBBING. The audience's attention is riveted on a night-club entertainer by a powerful spotlight beam. The eye gradu-ally grows accustomed to this, but the camera must be used skil-fully for a good picture. In this case, the picture was strengthened by the concentration on a limited area, leaving unwanted detail in total shadow. The camera: Canon with f/1.9 Serenar. The ex-posure: 1/25 second at f/8, on Plus-X film. The singer: Carmen McRae, in New York's Basin Street.

CHAPTER 6

SPORTS, SPECIAL EVENTS AND PROJECTS

- - - More Available-Light Subjects and Techniques

Sports "Under The Lights"

Most of the sport pictures we see in newspapers and magazines are made in broad daylight or with flashbulbs or electronic flash. The fact that sports mean *action* has tended to prejudice photographers and editors in favor of brilliant lighting.

Here, if anywhere, sunlight and flash have real justification. The thing that arrests us in a great sport picture is that we can see things in it that we could not really have seen if we had been at the event. The human eye and its image-registering function do not operate rapidly enough for us to get a true view of the fighter's grimace under a swift left hook, or the sprinter's expression as he breaks the tape. We get a fleeting impression of these things, mixed with all the other things there are for the eye to see at such an instant. In the speedlight photograph, though, we can study these expressions and postures minutely.

This is a marvelous thing when it is done expertly. But there is also a place in sports work for available-light technique. More than any high-speed flash shot can, it can help recreate the atmosphere of the whole event, more or less as the eye sees it.

There are dozens of magnificent sports pictures waiting to be made with available light. Here are three examples. One has already been done, the other two probably haven't.

— A set showing a losing football team filing through a stadium exit after twilight.

— A set capturing action peaks in track events: the pole-vaulter at the top of his leap, the hurdler in full stride, etc.

— A set analyzing the remarkable dance-like motion of basketball players excuting a tricky play.

Here are some specific tips on available-light shooting in particular sports situations.

Basketball

A basketball court is so well lighted that it would be a Class II situation, if it were not for the fast pace of the action involved. Always, the best shots are to be had at the moments of the maddest scrambles for the ball, the sprinting dribble down the sidelines.

The place for a camera without flash on the basketball court is behind the basket, or somewhere along the ends of the playing area as close as possible to the basket. Avoid the sides of the court; shooting from there heightens the effect of fast motion, as players cross your field of view at right angles.

There are two things to keep in mind:

1. Peak action
2. Direction of motion (it should be straight toward you)

Taking both of these factors into consideration, with a shutter speed of 1/25 second, you should be able to get an exciting shot just as a player pushes the ball into the basket. If your lens and the lighting permit you to shoot faster, by all means do so.

And if your camera has a fairly slow lens, don't ignore the possibility of getting some fine motion-blur studies showing the poise and grace of the game. Shoot as slow as you must, but remember the limitation imposed by camera steadiness. You don't want camera shake to add to (or cancel out) the subject motion. If you are shooting slower than your own steadiness permits, brace the camera on a solid support.

70

SPORTS ACTION, NO FLASH. Here is a fine example of rapid motion stopped under available light, without an extremely high shutter speed. Durniak caught this interesting basketball activity at an Iowa high school tournament. He used a twin-lens reflex and Super-XX film, and shot at 1/100 second, f/3.5. Development was rather unorthodox: he used DK-50 (usually recommended for larger film sizes), and four times the normal immersion time.

Bob Schwalberg

IN THE RING. When action demands a fast shutter speed, good available-light technique can make it possible. Here Schwalberg photographed fighter Tuzo Portuguez in an actual bout at 1/250 second, f/2.8, using a 35-mm Nikon and Ilford HP-3 film, which he processed for 14 minutes in Promicrol. This was an effective film speed rating of about ASA 400.

Indoor Track Events

Lighting on an indoor track is generally more dispersed than on a boxing ring or a basketball court, so most of the situations will be correspondingly more difficult. Don't try shooting a track meet until you have succeeded with some other kind of indoor sport.

Here, a lot depends on your familiarity with the action that takes place in each event, and sometimes on the particular style of the athlete. In events where straight running is involved, the factor of angle of motion is of prime importance. Place yourself where you can shoot at a shallow angle — that is, as nearly as possible in the same direction as the motion.

In hurdles, your best bet is to crouch alongside a hurdle and shoot at right angles. At shutter speeds too slow to stop the action, you will get beautiful flowing images of the runners' forms as they stretch out for the leap. The same is true for the broad jump, especially if you place yourself at the point of take-off or the expected landing spot.

The pole-vault and high jump are events in which peak action is the most important factor — since you can't choose an ideal camera angle. For pole-vault, use a long-focus lens if you can; the "high spot" will be 12 to 15 feet off the ground, and with an ordinary lens the jumper might be lost in the picture.

When it comes to weight-throwing, as in the hammer-toss, shotput, discus and javelin throws, watch for the poised instant just before the release of energy, and for the moment after release when the body has completed its follow-through.

In The Squared Circle

There is usually a lot of light in a boxing arena, and most of it is concentrated on those few square feet of canvas outlined by heavy ropes. It's all overhead light, but it is well distributed on all sides, so you don't need to worry about any side of a boxer being in shadow — unless it's in the shadow of one of the other two men in the ring.

If you're shooting workouts or preliminary bouts, and you know someone who knows the management, you should be able to get into the ring before the fighting starts, but with all the lights on, to take some exposure meter readings. Take one from a spot fully exposed to all the lights, and another from your hand held in the shadow of your body; the latter will guide you when the action is close-in, and faces and fists are shadowed.

The clinches are interesting moments for available-light shooting, and they're largely ignored by press cameramen who are always looking for a knockout blow that will make a front-page picture. In a clinch, movement is largely stopped, but there is often tremendous tension visible in the faces and muscles of the fighters.

Boxing is another sport in which a motion-blur interpretation of the fast action can be an arresting photograph, almost an abstraction. There's an interesting box-camera project: load with fast film and catch a whole flurry of blows in a short "bulb" exposure.

Get as close as you can to ringside, of course; use a long-focus lens if you're more than a couple of rows back. And above all, watch for those peaks of action. There's an instant of stopped motion just as a solid blow lands that makes it possible for even a 1/5-second shutter to get a picture — if the man behind the camera is alert enough to catch it.

Shoot A Wedding

Have you ever watched a "candid" wedding photographer at work, with a 4x5 press camera, a flashgun with extensions manned by a pair of assistants, and a small trunkful of gear? And have you looked at the album he delivers? A record of a wedding is a priceless possession, but one wonders sometimes that the bride and groom and the wedding party are willing to pay such a price!

Flashbulbs have a way of giving a wedding the air of a movie premiere or a press conference, rather than a dignified and moving occasion. How much more fitting it is to cover the marriage ceremony and its preparations and parties with the unobtrusive available-light camera. Nowhere else is it so appropriate to record the dignity and splendor of an event without disturbing its natural feeling.

If there is to be a wedding in your family or among your friends, take advantage of what you have learned about available light to

WITH A MODEST CAMERA. The smiling bride was photographed by an amateur using a Kodak Monitor 620 roll-film folding camera, which has an f/4.5 lens — proving that high-priced glassware is not always necessary for success with available light. Here, most of the illumination came from a pair of small boudoir lamps, a little from the window. The exposure was 1/25 second at f/4.5, on Super-XX film.

make a distinctive picture story of it. Before the ceremony, follow the movements of either bride or groom, whomever is more accessible to you. You can't cover both effectively at once, and it's better to have a complete record of one.

Go with the bride as she chooses her gown, as she prepares lists for invitations, at the shower (if you are permitted), and in the hectic hours just before the ceremony.

Or go with the groom as he is fitted at the tailor's, as he selects a gift for his best man, at the stag party, and in *his* hectic and nervous last hours as a bachelor.

Try to visit the church in advance, to familiarize yourself with the situation and take some meter readings. Be sure that lighting conditions are as they will be for the wedding. Your picture-taking during the ceremony will depend on what is acceptable and proper. If you cannot be near the altar during the wedding itself, probably you can arrange to shoot during a rehearsal.

Your real mission begins as the couple emerges from the church. Shoot quickly then without interrupting them to pose; concentrate on the mood of the moment. Adjust exposure fast, for shooting into the dark interior of their car.

The reception will probably be a typical party situation, as far as photography is concerned. Refer to the notes on party shooting in an earlier chapter.

Follow through with pictures of the couple moving into their new home, and you will have an album that will be their most treasured wedding gift.

Special Projects For Available Light

The preceding pages have discussed the approach to many common situations with available-light technique. Here are some ideas for photo projects specially suited to small camera work with high film speeds. They will suggest many more, related to your own life and experience.

A book of portraits of the people in your school or office.

A documentary record of your business. For instance, the operation of a small manufacturing plant, from raw material to finished products.

A time-and-motion study of industrial operations, to reveal weak spots and suggest improvements.

A record of a child's growth, month by month, in relation to one home situation: at the table, in the bath, with pencil or chalk, etc.

"Pets without flash" — a warm "adventure story," perhaps, starring your dog or cat.

A commuter's travels, in car and train; an important part of America's transportation picture.

A day in the life of a family. A picture story, made preferably on a rainy weekend when everyone is at home and staying indoors.

PSEUDO AVAILABLE LIGHT. Electronic flash helped make this charming shot of a little girl's kitchen apprenticeship. The speedlight was aimed at the light-colored ceiling to supplement existing daylight in the room, making possible an exposure at f/11 on Super-XX film, which was developed for 20 minutes in DK-50. The camera was a 35-mm Voigtlander Vito. Note the soft, nondirectional quality of light obtained with this technique. Photoflood can be used this way, too.

CHAPTER 7

NOT QUITE AVAILABLE LIGHT

- - - How To Use Indirect Flash and Flood Without Losing Available-Light Quality

Strictly speaking, available-light means just what it says: no illumination of any kind except that existing in a given situation. But not so strictly speaking, it is possible to introduce additional light in the form of flash or flood in such a way that the situation is not disturbed, and the resulting pictures cannot be distinguished from those made with available-light alone.

This is done in two ways, for two different purposes:

1. A small amount of bounce flash, which is just enough to bring an impossible situation within the realm of the possible. This changes the exposure by only a stop or two.

2. A pre-arranged set-up of bounce flood or flash, which changes the whole situation as far as exposure is concerned, though it does not alter the naturalness or spontaneity of the situation.

Bounce Light

The first method is now widely used by non-purist professionals (and few can afford to be purists these days). Most of them use small and very portable electronic flash units, aiming the reflector directly at the ceiling above the subject or at an adjacent wall. Sometimes the reflector is tilted forward slightly, to "spill" some direct light on the subject. No very useful guide can be given for exposures with this method, since there are too many variables, and the increment in light is so subtle. Exposure with bounce light depends on the intensity of the flash, the color of walls and ceiling, the distance from flash to ceiling to subject — and of course the amount of light originally present. This is largely a trial-and-error method; you might experiment by using a shutter speed twice as fast as indicated by a meter reading.

A sidelight: one top *Life* photojournalist makes portraits by this technique, with a specially designed reflector that has a tiny hole in the side toward the subject; this permits enough light to "leak" through to put catchlights in his subject's eyes.

Boosting Room Light

The other technique, which amounts to changing the quantity but not the quality of illumination, is well adapted to parties, playrooms, workshops, and family pictures. Ideally, it consists of replacing one or more of the room's usual light sources with a flash or flood bulb in a reflector, directed at a wall or ceiling. In this case there are some suggestions to be made about exposure. Here is a table, based on the use of a fast pan film (about 200 ASA), in an average size room with medium-gray walls and ceiling, and a total lamp-to-subject distance of 8 or 10 feet.

WITH FLASH

AG-1 or M-2 bulb	1/50 sec, f/5.6
No. 5, 25, or M-5 bulb	1/50 sec, f/8
No. 40 bulb	1/50 sec, f/11
No. 22 bulb	1/100 sec, f/16

WITH FLOOD

1 No. 1 photoflood	1/25 sec, f/2.8
2 No. 1 photoflood	1/25 sec, f/3.5
1 RFL-2 or RSP-2 bulb*	1/25 sec, f/3.5
2 RFL-2 or RSP-2 bulbs*	1/25 sec, f/4.5
1 No. 2 photoflood	1/25 sec, f/4.5
2 No. 2 photofloods	1/25 sec, f/5.6

*RFL and RSP bulbs are funnel-shaped lamps with built-in silvered reflectors.

Harvey Shaman

WHEN YOU ADD BOUNCE FLOOD. An effect generally identical to that of avail-able-light can be achieved by bouncing photoflood illumination from walls and ceilings. With active children who like to move into dark corners as well as light ones, it's a good idea to raise the light level in the whole room. The bounce technique avoids the harshness of direct flood. This shot was made with a 35-mm Nikon, and two floods supplemented window light.

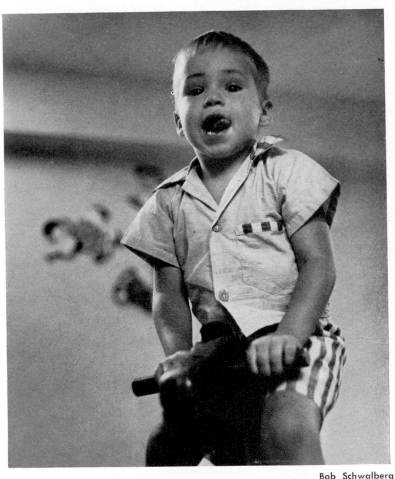

FLOODLIGHT FOR FAST ACTION. A single photoflood lamp, directed at the ceiling, permitted the photographer to shoot at 1/500 second, f/2.8 stopping the furious motion of a boy on a spring-mounted horse. Tri-X film was rated at about ASA 1,600, and development was for 14 minutes in Promicrol. This is a case of taking the fullest advantage of the latitude of the film-and-developer combination to work at high speeds. The camera was a 2.8C Rolleiflex.

This table, of course, gives only base exposures. You can increase shutter speed if you open the aperture correspondingly, and decrease it if you stop down. In using more than one bulb, you cannot usually figure on fully doubling or tripling speed, since additional light sources will generally be placed as fill-in or backlight, or too far from the subject to be as effective as the main light source.

There are a few pictures in this book which were made with supplementary "available-type" light, both flood and flash. Notice that all of these, without exception, are indistinguishable from true available-light shots; only the captions betray the secret.

There is a variation of this technique which is applicable to many home situations. You can replace the usual light bulbs in lamps and fixtures with larger ones — not floods, but ordinary bulbs. If you can replace, for instance, a 100-watt bulb in an indirect lamp with a 200-watt one, you can make party or playtime shooting a lot easier for yourself.

Albert Gruen

CHAPTER 8

FROM CAMERA
TO FINISHED PRINT

How to Develop and Print Your Own Available-Light Pictures

It's Not All In The Shooting

A lot depends on what happens after you make the last shot on a roll of film. If you're serious about your picture-taking, that exposed and undeveloped roll of film in your hand is a precious possession. You're not going to trust it to a stranger, any more than you would trust a fine watch to an unknown repairman.

If you know someone — a lab or an individual — who does good custom processing and is willing to follow your instructions, you are fortunate. Even in large cities, however, there are not many such competent processors who will handle non-professional work.

You read in an earlier chapter that it is highly preferable to do your own film developing, as well as extremely easy. Even though you may have to trust your print-making to someone else, there is no reason why you should not process all your own film, right from the beginning — and there are these reasons why you *should*:

IN A DARK DOORWAY. Fine printing preserved the long tonal range, from black background to whites of eyes and earring highlights. Here the camera penetrated into deep shadow, obtaining a fine exposure for flesh tones, ignoring everything else, so that even the hair is completely invisible. Though the lighting is flat, there is excellent modeling of the features. A Rolleiflex was used, at 1/25 second, f/4, on Super-XX film.

1.   You can control your results, learn from your mistakes, and correct your errors, as you do in shooting.

2.   It is less than one-tenth as expensive.

3.   It is faster; you see your negatives within a half hour.

4.   It is enormously satisfying to "follow through" on the pictures you have taken.

The two old arguments against doing your own developing are easily countered:

"It's too much bother!" Might as well say it's too much bother to prepare a fresh-caught rainbow trout for the skillet, or to install a new power tool in the home workshop. It's part of the fun.

"I haven't got a darkroom or equipment!" You've already read how it's possible to develop film with no darkroom at all, and a minimum of equipment. Here again is all you need:

FACILITIES
> A dark closet
> A kitchen sink, or equivalent

EQUIPMENT
> Developing tank
> Tank thermometer
> Funnel, cellulose sponge (*optional*)

SUPPLIES
> Developer
> Fixer
> Stop bath, wetting agent (*optional*)

Time-and-Temperature Developing

As for the basic procedure, you have already learned it or you can find it in an elementary handbook. There is a brief run-through of it earlier in this book.

Beyond the "basic," however, lies most of what's important in available-light processing. For instance, if you were to shoot a roll of film under adverse light conditions, following exposure suggestions made in this book, and then develop it as the manufacturer recommends, you would be almost assured of disappointment.

It can't be stressed too strongly that success in available-light technique depends on *the proper combination of exposure and development*. Some examples of such proper combinations are shown in a table elsewhere in this book.

These are only intended as guides to your own experimentation. If you find they don't match your own experience, it doesn't mean that either you or the table is wrong. It means only that there is more than one way of being right.

There are so many variables and individual factors in this specialized kind of photography that no absolute rules can ever be conveyed from one person to another. There is a difference in the way we interpret exposure meters, timing devices, even thermometers. There is a difference in the way we "give the benefit of the doubt" when a question arises. And, finally, there are differences in what each of us will call a "good" result.

Fortunately, modern films and chemicals have two characteristics that help reduce this difficulty. One is their *consistency*; once you achieve perfection in processing, you can repeat your performance at will. Another is their *latitude*, their "margin for error." But in available light we are already exploiting this factor to the extreme, so we cannot expect it to cover any serious deviations.

There are just three principal aims in available-light processing:

DENSITY — enough to give an easily printable image.

DETAIL — in both shadows and highlights.

FINE GRAIN — as fine as possible.

The real issue is this: How far can you exploit the speed-increasing qualities of your film-and-developer combination, and still preserve high quality?

This question of quality is a subjective one, dependent on your own definition. You may be interested in maximum speed at all costs; you may insist on shadow detail at the expense of speed; you may hate coarse grain more than anything else. Here is an example, based on experiments by Bob Schwalberg.

Suppose you take two rolls of 35-mm Plus-X, and expose them identically, then process them to the point where they have identical shadow density, one in Promicrol, and the other in D-76 — both very good developers for available-light work. The Promicrol roll will show less density and more detail in the *highlights*, finer grain, and less tendency to fog than the D-76 roll.

But if what you want is greatest shadow density (what you might call "the most image for your money") you can go much further with D-76 and its borax-supercharged cousin D-76F.

This leads professionals to the conclusion that when using 35-mm Plus-X with Promicrol, your best working film speed is ASA 320; with D-76, it is 200. (Note that these figures do not hold for rollfilm Plus-X.)

Developers

In the developing guide chart in this book you will find three developers mentioned (apart from Dektol, which is essentially a print developer, used for film only in emergencies). These are by no means the only good ones, but they offer a point of reference and a standard of comparison. All three are energetic fine-grain formulae.

D-23

D-23 is a developer you can't buy ready-mixed. But nothing could be simpler, or cheaper, than mixing it yourself: only two chemicals and water are required. The formula is available from Kodak.

When grain shows up on D-23 negatives, it is not sharp and clear, but soft and indistinct. Some people prefer this grain quality, feeling that it is likely to be less objectionable to the untrained eye; others would rather have their grain sharp and "honest." This latter group uses D-23 too, because it minimizes contrast and resists blocking-up (loss of detail) at the extremes of highlight and shadow. It is known to offer the broadest exposure-and-development latitude, especially in combination with Tri-X film.

D-76

D-76 is a pre-mixed packaged developer with such excellent qualities for small-camera processing that it has become something of a standard, against which other formulae are measured and compared.

Maynard Frank Wolfe

A MAN AND HIS WORK. This picture was developed in Microdol followed by D-76. With strong sidelighting from a window, the camera caught the writer at his desk, giving good modeling to the features on one side of the face, and leaving the other side in shadow for emphasis. Wolfe used a twin-lens reflex and Plus-X film at 1/25 second, f/4.

LIGHTING FOR DRAMA. Here, Tri-X film was developed in PRA-400. Facing his subject directly toward a window, Wolfe shot a strong profile in which all unnecessary detail is suppressed, and a completely natural feeling is achieved by simple lighting. The camera was a twin-lens reflex, exposure 1/50 second at f/3.5.

(This is by no means the same as saying that any one developer is *best*). It produces sharp, crisp grain, in contrast to the soft grain of D-23. When film is developed in it for more than the 13 or 15 minutes recommended in the table, there is some increase in grain and a heightening of contrast, with blocking (lack of detail) in highlights. This is an example of the reasons why you must not give extra development time for "good measure." When you shoot a "mixed" roll, with daylight and available-light exposures on the same piece of film, you should rate the outdoor exposures at almost twice the recommended speed, about ASA 400 to avoid blocking-up. This does not apply to Tri-X, however; only to Plus-X and similar films.

Promicrol

Promicrol is an imported product, made in England, and it has had wide acceptance for available-light work because of its resistance to fog and to blanking out of highlights, and because of its grain quality, which is finer than that of D-76. It does not have quite the latitude of D-23 for overexposure and overdevelopment, so be sure to expose and process within the table's recommendations. Again, with a mixed roll, you should double the speed rating for the daylight shots, except with Tri-X. Promicrol's contrast characteristics are somewhere between those of D-23 and D-76 — greater contrast than with D-23 and less than with D-76. As far as grain is concerned, it permits you to work with Tri-X at about ASA 650 and get only a little more grain than you would with Plus-X at 320 — and with considerably better quality, because of Tri-X's improved shadow density and lower contrast.

Note that with Tri-X, you shoot at exactly the same speeds for D-76 as for Promicrol, but that development time is slightly less for the latter. With the other films, Promicrol offers almost twice the speed.

There are three other developers — two new and one an old-timer — that are worth some discussion for their particular application to available-light processing.

Microphen

Microphen, like Promicrol, is a British import, manufactured by Ilford, makers of HP-3 and other films. Tests have shown its performance to be comparable to that of Promicrol at advanced film-speed ratings, and it has certain advantages. It offers greater latitude, both in exposure and development time. It can "push" film further, by extended development, without highlight blocking and increase in grain. (For example, it has given satisfactory results with Tri-X film at an effective speed of ASA 5,000, with 16-minute immersion.) And its "keeping" qualities are much better than Promicrol's — a factor which made the earlier product economically impractical for some amateurs.

Ethol UFG

This is an ultra-fine-grain developer with a temperature tolerance from 60 to 90°F — a distinct advantage when you can't control your darkroom temperature easily. Bob Schwalberg's recommendation for elevated speed ratings with UFG are: Tri-X and HP-3 — 6 to 8 minutes for 650-800 ASA; HP-S — 7 to 9 minutes for 800-1000 ASA. (Based on normal temperature of 68-70°F with intermittent agitation.)

Acufine

This is the latest entrant in the developer derby, introduced in mid-1961. It is clearly the most remarkable chemical of its kind, enabling you to rate Tri-X at ASA 1200; HP-S, Isopan Record, and Super Hypan at 1000; and HP-3 at 500 — all with a degree of image quality that would be hard to match with anything else. In a demonstration, Bill Pierce exposed Tri-X at 4800 ASA and got an admittedly thin negative which nevertheless permitted a 24-times blow-up suitable for magazine reproduction! Development times are given in great detail in the manufacturer's leaflet; they are generally much shorter than for other developers. Typical: for Tri-X at 1200, at 70°F: 4 minutes, 45 seconds.

After the Developer

Should you use a stop bath, which is listed in the table as "optional"? The answer is yes. You don't need it, but it does help preserve your fixing bath and promote uniformity of results. It's cheap enough to be discarded after use, if you don't have room to store it, and it's almost as easy to use as the repeated water rinse you must otherwise use.

Gottlieb Wittwer, from Popular Photography Picture Contest:

WHEN WEATHER'S BAD. The proper combination of exposure and development is a necessity in obtaining such high quality from difficult shots. A cloudy sky with snow or rain in the air can turn an ordinary outdoor scene into a difficult available-light problem. This prize-winning picture required a reflex camera's maximum aperture of f/3.5, even with fast Ilford HP-3 film and the moderate shutter speed of 1/50 second. Wittwer made the shot on a street corner in Zurich, Switzerland, at six o'clock on a winter evening.

Albert Gruen

The fixing bath should contain a hardener, for the preservation and protection of negatives. Almost everyone now uses a rapid fixer, which cuts immersion time to about five minutes.

Inspection Development

All the discussion about processing so far in this book has been based on the time-and-temperature method of development, the temperature being uniformly 68°F, and the time varying as indicated in the tables; this is the method which makes possible film processing without a darkroom. It is undeniably attractive to the amateur without lab facilities, and it is unquestionably a "lazy man's" method — which is recommendation enough.

But there is another method, used by all custom processing labs and all meticulous professionals: development by inspection. This means just what it says. You watch the film while it develops, and stop the process when density and contrast are right, instead of waiting until it's all over and wishing you had stopped sooner.

Needless to say, inspection development is a special skill that is developed with practice, but you don't have to be a genius to master it. If possible, you should learn it from someone who knows how, because the qualities of emergent images on film are difficult to interpret.

Here's the way to teach yourself inspection development, if you must learn by yourself. Get a standard green safelight, and place it at least three feet from your working space. Some professionals choose to replace the normal bulb with a smaller one, to reduce the danger of fogging the film. Determine the normal development time — whatever you would use for the time-and-temperature method. Two

_____

OUT-OF-FOCUS BACKGROUND. This was developed by inspection. Sometimes an unrelated background can be made to add something to a picture, if it is thrown out of sharp focus and falls into place in the composition. This little boy was caught at play on a dining room rug, and the window, table, and chairs behind him do not distract. A twin-lens reflex was used at its maximum aperture, f/3.5, and focus was sharp on the child's face. Film was Super-XX, shutter speed 1/10 second, development in PRA-400.

or three minutes before the time is up, remove the film from the tank and examine the emulsion side by the dim green light. Keep it three feet away from the film! Return it to the tank, no matter what the image looks like to you, and complete the "normal" development. Fix, rinse, and inspect by white light. Then you will be able to determine whether a longer or shorter immersion time would have been better. After you have practiced in this way a few times, begin to let your experience guide you in actually shortening or lengthening the time.

If you use the inspection technique constantly, you will soon learn to "read" negatives accurately, and the quality of your work will improve. The subleties of inspection development are a matter for extensive discussion; it has been frequently treated in other books and in magazine articles.

Intensification?

Some of your available-light pictures will inevitably suffer from the fact that there just wasn't enough light available. These negatives need not be considered a total loss. The images can be built up to a certain degree by the use of intensifiers, of which there are many kinds available. Your photo dealer can recommend one. Use it on one negative at a time, for better control, and to avoid spoiling others.

There is another process called latensification (short for latent-image-intensification), by which density can be increase after exposure but *before* development. But be sure you don't use it unnecessarily, or you will have the effect of overexposure. The process is described in specialized technical literature.

Of course, the object in available-light technique is to get good pictures by proper use of the film-and-developer combination itself, and this is possible today in almost any conceivable situation. Don't become dependent on intensification; go back and try to take fuller advantage of the latitude of your film and your developer.

Great Care Pays Off

From the moment you break the seal on an exposed roll of film, or open the 35-mm cartridge, until the moment you've slipped the finished negatives into protective envelopes, you're vulnerable to all kinds of enemies of picture perfection. As if it weren't enough that your developing time might be a little off, or your fixing time insufficient, you have two more nasty factors to contend with: dust and scratches.

Dust on the film before it goes into the developer can actually become a part of the image — a speck that will eventually mean spotting of the finished print. Work in a dust-free place when loading the tank; if you use a closet, see that it is free of lint and loose dust before you begin.

Foreign matter in the developer can have the same unfortunate effect. Filter all solutions after use, so they will be free of sediment next time you need them.

Fingers are the handiest of tools, but they must be kept in their place through the whole processing operation. Without exception, their place is on the *edges* of the film. Fingernails can inadvertently scratch the emulsion, and part of your picture is gone forever. Perspiration can etch a fingerprint permanently into the emulsion or even the film base.

In wiping excess water from the finished negatives, never use anything but a fine-textured cellulose sponge or a soft chamois. A wetting agent, such as Kodak Photo-Flo, used after the final rinse, can eliminate or reduce the necessity for wiping off excess water; it prevents the water from collecting in droplets on the film surface.

Hang negatives to dry in a place that is dust-free and where they will not be disturbed. When cutting them apart for storage, take great care with scissors and avoid touching anything except the edges. Don't store more than one strip of film in a single envelope; the corners of one strip can scratch the surface of the others.

In enlarging, don't use a negative carrier in which the film must be slid through a channel; there is too much danger of dust and grit becoming lodged in the channel. Remove the carrier each time you move to a new frame.

Meticulous care all along the way — even bordering on the fanatical — will pay off in clean prints and a valuable negative collection.

Tiny scratches — which you will almost inevitably get in spite of all warnings — can be filled in enough so they will not show on the print, by using a very thin application of petroleum jelly on the film base. Apply it with a fingertip just lightly coated with the jelly.

The Print's The Thing

The last step in the photographic process is a crucial one. All your effort is wasted unless the end product is a fine print. Volumes have been written on printing and print quality; photo magazines discuss it repeatedly; beginners' books generally give sound outlines of printing technique. Still, thousands of amateurs have yet to make a really good print. The fact is that there is more to it than can be taught by any book or magazine.

The first step is to recognize and agree upon what good print quality is. As nearly as can be described in words, it is something like this: a good print contains rich blacks and crisp, pure highlights, with a broad range of intermediate gray tones. It has no areas of blank white totally lacking in detail, except of course in a subject that is completely smooth, lacking both form and texture. This means, for instance, that a man's white shirt should have ample detail, in its folds and wrinkles and stitching. A good print has no areas of black totally lacking in detail, unless, again, the subject or the mood demands it. Thus a black flannel suit should have detail and texture, unless there is a reason for not wanting it.

This is not the place for a treatise on enlarging. But good printing technique is especially important in available-light work, because negatives are often far from ideal, and difficult to print well. It is probably true, too, that poor printing is more objectionable in available-light work than elsewhere, for it heightens and calls attention to the faults we try so hard to correct: excessive contrast, lack of detail, fuzziness, grain, and (though it may seem to contradict the excessive contrast) a certain gray flatness inherent in some thin negatives exposed in dull light.

Harvey Shaman

PRODUCER'S PORTRAIT. Allen Funt, famed for his Candid Micro-
phone and Candid Camera on radio and television, was photographed by window light alone, with a twin-lens reflex. Shaman
chose his camera angle carefully, so that some of the daylight
would spill onto the shadow side of the face. Inclusion of the
hands makes a great contribution to this portrait's success, as
do the details in his clothing.

99

Albert Gruen

LOW-KEY PORTRAITURE AND DODGING. "Low-key" means an emphasis on the dark tones; it is a product both of lighting and exposure, and the effect can be heightened in printing. Some poor light situations lend themselves well to low-key treatment. This portrait was made under a fluorescent light about six feet above the subject. Exposure was on the short side: 1/25 second at f/3.5 with a Rolleiflex, and no "pushing" for added film speed was employed. Considerable dodging was done to hold detail and texture in face and hand.

Printing Difficult Negatives

The following paragraphs contain a few valuable suggestions and tips that apply to the printing of available-light pictures.

Insure absolute rigidity of the enlarger. Don't allow any unsharpness to enter at the printing stage. Use an easel which holds the paper really flat.

Focus on the grain. Many amateurs deceive themselves by giving the focusing knob an extra little twist and making the grain disappear. This naturally makes image sharpness disappear too. If grain is of the sharp type, it makes an easier target than any part of the image itself.

Standardize your materials in printing just as you do in shooting. Settle on one combination of paper and developer that works well for you, and don't switch without some very good reason.

If you're not now using a variable-contrast enlarging paper, give it a try. In available-light work, where some of the knottiest problems are those of contrast, you need at least two or three grades of paper on hand, and the variable-contrast variety can mean real economy, in spite of the extra investment for the necessary filters.

It is a good idea to use a paper with the developer recommended by the manufacturer, but it's not an inflexible rule. For example, a combination favored by many professionals is DuPont's Varigam with Kodak's Dektol developer.

A couple of reminders that apply to any kind of printing: Allow the paper its full time in the developer, usually about two minutes. If you find yourself "yanking" (removing the print to soon) or "pushing" (leaving it in too long), adjust the enlarger exposure time. Unless your negative is uncommonly dense, stop down the enlarger lens to extend exposure time; it's easier to figure a ten-percent increase in a 20-second exposure than in a 4-second one.

Learn to dodge skilfully. Two of the most valuable tools for handling uneven negatives are the burning-in of highlights and the holding back of shadows. The human hand will always be the most versatile dodging instrument, but you can always use bits of cardboard or paper on wire for small areas.

MOTION BLUR. This shot of a broad-jumper in mid-leap shows how a little less sharpness in an action photograph can heighten the feeling of movement. If the jumper had been completely "frozen" with electronic flash, the result might be fascinating, but it would not be a picture of action itself, as this one is. Wolfe got this picture during an athletic competition in Madison Square Garden, New York, using a Canon at its maximum aperture of f/1.9, which permitted a shutter speed of 1/100 second on Tri-X film.

CHAPTER 9

ERRORS WITH AVAILABLE LIGHT

- - - Even You Can Make Mistakes!

Four fundamental things can make available-light pictures less than perfect:

> Overexposure plus overdevelopment
>
> Underexposure
>
> Grain
>
> Motion blur

It might occur to you that these are marks of failure in every kind of photography. True, but these four are the ones that cause the most havoc when light is poor. No matter which of them plagues your own available-light shooting, there is something you can do to help.

The Paradox: Too Much Light

It's funny, but more available-light pictures are ruined by overexposure than by underexposure. This is due largely to a pesky phenomenon that causes a lot of trouble in other areas of life too: human nature.

Confronted with a situation in which there is not as much light as desired, the all-too-human photographer will try to compensate by adding exposure. He will do this no matter what his exposure meter tells him.

And, faced with a roll of film he knows was shot under adverse conditions, he will develop it for a couple of extra minutes "just to be sure." He will do this no matter how many experts are breathing down his neck.

This interesting twin sin amounts to compounding an error. The equation he now has is not overexposure added to overdevelopment, but overexposure *multiplied* by overdevelopment. If he had made only one mistake — either one — his negatives might be satisfactorily printable. But with both mistakes his problem is beyond solution, in terms of a quality result.

The primary symptom of the disease is a total blankness of high-light areas. He has sacrificed all detail there in order to get some in the shadows, which he was worried about. This has happened because of a characteristic of developers: they work much more rapidly in highlight areas than in shadows. Exposure has been perhaps twice as long as it should have been, so this unevenness of developing action is even more pronounced.

Shadow areas may have a little more detail than they would have had otherwise, but the total effect is unfortunate. And the added development time has contributed to another misfortune: graininess.

Remedy

The solution to the problem is simple enough, if you've learned your lesson. Accept your meter reading at face value, for whatever effective film-speed rating you have chosen. And develop for no longer than the times suggested in the charts in the back of this book. Some situations, particularly those in which light comes from a very strong single source, will cause more trouble than others when overexposed. These cases will have to be dealt with by burning-in and holding-back in enlargement.

There are some pictures in this book which could be considered examples of the error of overexposure and overdevelopment. They have been included partly for this very reason, and partly because they happen to be good pictures in spite of the fault. Spot the errors, and learn from them. Notice too the numerous pictures (especially in the portrait category) in which exposure and processing were just right, producing a wide range of tonal values with no blocking of highlights or shadows.

WHAT IS "TOO MUCH" CONTRAST? When there is strong light from a single source, excessive contrast is almost always the result. But in this case the photographer felt that the strong black and white opposition in the face of this horse-show rider was a virtue rather than a fault. The face has a mask-like quality, and attention is riveted on the center of interest. The camera was a Contax, film Plus-X, exposure 1/25 second at f/1.5, development in Microdol and D-76.

ONLY A SHAFT OF SUNLIGHT. A sensitive portrait of famed dancer Harald Kreutzberg was made in Salzburg, Austria. Though it is not an indoor picture, the nature of the illumination makes it a difficult available-light job, but notice the fine detail from the shadowed chin to the highlighted brow. Most of the dancer's face was in the deep shadow of a building and his arm; only a ray of direct sun fell across his forehead. Okamoto used a Rolleiflex and Ilford HP-3 film, shot at 1/250 second, f/11.

What You Might Expect: Too Little Light

Underexposure is found on the negatives of two kinds of photographers:

The beginner who thought he could shoot in semi-darkness the way he shot in daylight, and

The experienced worker who has simply tried and failed in a very difficult situation.

The symptom, of course, is an extraordinary blackness of everything in the print — with perhaps a dark-grayness of some highlight areas.

Remedy

For the tyro, of course, the cure is simply to learn a few of the fundamentals of available-light technique, and stop wasting film.

The professional or advanced amateur who suffers from chronic underexposure in situations where others are getting better results may find that he is a little too cautious in his technique. Presumably he is using his maximum aperture, but he may not trust himself to work at shutter speeds that are slow enough.

Practice builds confidence in your ability to shoot at 1/10 and 1/5 second, and even at $\frac{1}{2}$ second with a little support. Remember, moving your shutter speed down just one notch will give you 100% more exposure.

Be sure you are getting all the speed out of your film-and-developer combination that is consistent with good-quality results.

This is probably the place to admit that there will be some cases of underexposure which could only be prevented by the acquisition of a faster lens. And, inevitably there will be some cases that cannot be prevented at all.

"Baseballs" On Your Negatives?

Fifteen years ago, when available-light photography was first gaining acceptance among working professionals, grain was almost fashionable. It had to be, because when you shot at a phenomenally high speed such as ASA 500, you got grain along with your speed.

Robert Frank, from Popular Photography Picture Contest

ALMOST AN EXTREME. This candid shot made at a carnival in Switzerland shows what a gifted photographer can do under near-impossible conditions. Light came from numerous small bulbs, all colored. Frank had to shoot at 1/20 second to stop motion in the carnival's confusion, and fortunately his Leica was equipped with the fast Japanese Nikkor f/1.4 lens, which he used wide open. The Plus-X film was processed for maximum image quality, with no special regard for fine grain.

Today we're a lot better off, thanks not only to new films and developers, but to the tireless and optimistic researches of a few working pros who have taught us to make best use of these new tools. We have begun to be a little snobbish now; we scorn the presence of noticeable grain in any but the most difficult of available-light pictures.

Graininess is the direct product of the vigor of the developer and the length of time the film is left in it (apart, of course, from the grain characteristics built into any particular film). People who insist on gaining speed by increasing development time are always going to have grain trouble.

Well-exposed negatives made in all available-light situations of Class I and Class II can be developed satisfactorily without any increase of grain at all. Most of those shot in Class III situations can be handled with a grain factor that is negligible to all but old-fashioned perfectionists.

Remedy

Choose a developer that is no more vigorous than required. Don't use SD-19a, for instance, when you can do perfectly well with D-76 or Promicrol. See the comparison of developers in table form at the end of this book.

Do not develop for a minute longer than the times suggested in the chapter on processing; perhaps with experience you can cut the time further. Every half-minute helps avoid increase in grain. These development times — please note — are generally shorter than those recommended by the manufacturers.

Things Happening Too Fast?

Everything moves at a rapid pace these days, and in photography we have learned to appreciate a little blur in a picture of moving objects to convey a sense of motion — just as cartoonists have always used "speed lines" to indicate that a figure is in motion. But beyond a certain point, this motion blur becomes just plain blur, and it gets in the way of our appreciation of the picture. Just where this point is, you must decide for yourself. It will be different, naturally, for different kinds of pictures.

When light is weak and you are using slow shutters, blur will be more troublesome than usual. But this is no reason to accept a blur that obscures the subject itself.

Remedy

Be sure you exhaust every possibility of using a faster shutter speed. Press your film-and-developer combination to exploit all the film's latitude. Use a wider aperture, if you have one.

Having determined what is the fastest shutter speed you can use, study the action for peaks — moments at which it is arrested, or points at which it moves toward you or away from you, rather than across your field of view. These are the instants at which you can get the most action-stopping value from any given shutter speed.

There is more specific information about peak-action shooting in the paragraphs about photographing basketball, boxing, and track events in *Chapter 6*.

COLOR FILM
AND AVAILABLE LIGHT

- - - Still Another Step Forward

When the first edition of this book was written, only a little over six years ago, the fastest color film had a speed of 32, and a few hardy alchemists were pushing it to 64. It was only with considerable reservation that available-light color could be suggested as possible.

The second edition, three years ago, said, "Now all that is changed, with the introduction of Super Anscochrome . . . " And all reference to the slower films was dropped. Well, now Super Anscochrome itself has been superseded, but it is by no means ruled out. Kodak's High Speed Ektachrome, Daylight Type, is rated at 160; Type B (balanced for studio floods) at 125. Super Anscochrome, in both types, was (and is) rated at 100.

You will choose the type that most nearly matches your available-light situation, of course. If most of the light is from the sky — daylight type; if mostly incandescent lamps — Tungsten or Type B. If you expect to encounter both types of light, yet want to limit yourself to a single film, your choice should be the Tungsten or Type B; either can be used in daylight with an 85B filter, though this reduces their speed to 80. The Daylight films don't convert faithfully to incandescent light sources.

The question uppermost in the available-lighter's mind is: Can I advance speed ratings with color as I can with black-and-white? And the answer, fortunately, is: Yes, but not so far. To rate them more than one stop faster than manufacturer's speeds is to take a chance on both image quality and color fidelity. Color processing laboratories are prepared to handle your film at advanced ratings, and will go further than one stop at your request. If you do not have such a specialized lab in your area, you might write to Kurshan & Lang, 10 East 46th St.; or Jack Ward Color Service, 202 East 44th St., both in New York City.

You can also process these films yourself, with kits and instructions provided by the manufacturers. Following is a guide to one-stop pushing of the two films already mentioned (in both types), and for Kodacolor negative material, which, with this advancement of speed, becomes an admissible available-light film. With these recommendations, you can give film one stop *less* exposure than normal.

Film	*Developing Time Increase*	
	First Dev.	*Color Dev.*
H. S. Ektachrome	3 min.	no change
Super Anscochrome	4 min.	5 min.
Kodacolor	4 min.	—

APPENDICES

I

TABLE OF SUGGESTED EXPOSURES
Based on actual meter readings in typical situations

In this book, available-light situations have been divided into three classes for purposes of reference and comparison (see *Chapter 4*). There is nothing precise about the limits of any one class, and most borderline situations could fall as logically into one class as another. However, this table can serve as a general guide to the kinds of shutter and aperture settings you might expect to use under typical conditions. Note that in each case only a base exposure is given; shutter speed and aperture can, of course, be adjusted for action, depth of field, or other reasons.

Films	Situations		
	CLASS I	CLASS II	CLASS III
Type 1 (ASA 125)	1/25 at f/3.5	1/10 at f/4	1/5 at f/2
Type 2 (ASA 200)	1/50 at f/3.5	1/25 at f/3.5	1/10 at f/2
Type 3 (ASA 400)	1/50 at f/5.6	1/50 at f/3.5	1/25 at f/2
Emergency Type 3 (ASA 800)	1/250 at f/2	1/100 at f/3.5	1/50 at f/2

DEVELOPING GUIDE

For 7 typical films, in 5 most-used developers

DEVELOPERS

FILMS	Acufine	UFG	Microphen	D-76	Promicrol
Plus-X (200-320)	3-4	3-4	7-9	7-8 (1:1)	7-9
FP-3 (160-200)	3-4	4-5	8-10	7-8	8-10
Record (1600-2400)	6-8	7-9			
HP-S (800-1000)	6-8	6-8	12-14	11-13	13-15
HP-3 (400-500)	3 3/4-4 3/4	4-5	10-12	8-10	9-11
Hypan (400-800)	6-8	4-5	10-12	8-10	9-11
Tri-X (400-800)	4-5	3½-4½	7-9	7-8	7-8

All times are for temperature of 70 F, with intermittent agitation.

III

HOW TO DETERMINE
YOUR OWN EXPOSURE INDEXES
AND DEVELOPING TIMES

by BILL PIERCE

Any available-light photographer, processing and printing his own work, will find it both easy and advantageous to compute "personalized" exposure indexes and developing times for his favorite film and developer combinations. While manufacturer's recommendations are accurate and almost always produce an acceptable photograph, they cannot take into account the personal variables of the way you use your meter or print a picture. They should serve only as a springboard for the photographic perfectionist who is willing to spend a little extra time to assure himself of the best possible technical results.

Your goal should be to arrive at an exposure index that will allow you to give a minimum exposure that will still retain all necessary shadow detail, and a development time that will give a negative of the correct contrast for printing on normal paper. Reason Number One: when shooting available light, it is always convenient to work with the highest possible exposure index (shortest exposure) compatible with top quality. Reason Number Two: the negative that such an exposure produces contains little or no excess density, and consequently is sharper and less grainy. Reason Number Three: when such a negative is of correct contrast, a top-quality print with full shadow and highlight detail is easier to achieve.

In order to arrive at these two numbers — index and development time — load your camera with a favorite film and select a shooting situation typical of those you record on this film. For instance, you might choose Tri-X Pan and a lamplit interior.

1. Set your meter at the manufacturer's recommended film speed (in this case, 400) and read the scene in your normal manner.

2. Take a series of bracketed exposures: one stop over (EI 200), as indicated (400), ½ stop under (640), one stop under (800), 1½ stops under (1200), and 2 stops under (1600).

3. Fire off a blank frame and repeat the sequence until you come to the end of the 35-mm roll. If using 120 rollfilm, it is best to expose three separate rolls.

4. Develop one of the 120 rolls, or a strip of about 15 inches of 35-mm film according to the manufacturer's recommendation. (If we chose D-76 for our Tri-X Pan, the time would be 7 min. at 68°F.) Label it for future identification. You will know the exposure index for each frame because they are in order between blank frames, the densest negative being the one shot at the lowest index.

5. Process the other two rolls, or two more strips, at 20 percent above and below the recommended times. (For Tri-X and D-76, this would be 5½ min. and 8½ min.) Label these also.

6. Make large prints (you will want to be able to see the grain) from each negative, discounting all negatives which are obviously unsatisfactory. Make all prints on your normal grade of paper from the same box. Change nothing from print to print except the exposure time needed to give the best possible straight print from each negative. On the back of each print note what negative it was made from, in terms of exposure index and development time.

7. Evaluate the prints and decide on the best one in terms of shadow detail, tone range, grain, and sharpness. On the back of this print you will have noted your "personalized" exposure index and development time.

INDEX

AVAILABLE LIGHT PHOTOGRAPHY

MEET THE AUTHOR

As managing editor—and formerly picture editor and feature editor of *Popular Photography*—"Mike" Kinzer has met and talked with thousands of professional and amateur photographers, among them some of the world's foremost exponents of the available-light technique. His specialty on the magazine has been to explain and simplify complex photographic ideas for its half-million readers. He has served as a judge in hundreds of picture contests, and as director of a gallery of photography. He is co-author with Fritz Henle of the book *Photography for Everyone*.

ABOUT THIS BOOK

A Special Kind of Photography

Here is *the* concise and crystal clear explanation of a special kind of photography—available light. This book tells you about the elements and techniques of this most convenient and natural type of photography—the small cameras, fast lenses and all speeds of available-light film. It explains and illustrates a variety of subjects under all conceivable available-light situations, both indoors and outdoors, from babies in the bath to night street scenes.

A Special Kind of Book

This is a special kind of book—it is half text and half illustrations. The text is accurate and to the point; it was written by a man highly respected by both professionals and amateurs. As a standard feature of all *Universal Photo Guides,* each fact in this book was rechecked for accuracy by a special technical editorial board.

The illustrations in this book were taken by a wide variety of people, from beginners in available-light photography to contest winners and working professionals. They used a wide variety of cameras, settings and developing procedures. Picture after picture in this book has a full caption showing the aperture, shutter-speed, focus settings and techniques used in shooting portraits, night scenes, children, parties, sports, mood scenes, etc. Thus you will actually *see* how to get the best results from available light, using the equipment, techniques and conditions you, the reader, will be using.

U-201   **Price $1.95**

COVER PHOTOGRAPHS
Basketball by John Durniak; *Night Scene* by Harvey Shaman; *Boy in Bath* by H. M. Kinzer; *Susan Strassberg* by Larry Fried (from Popular Photography Picture contest)

UNIVERSAL PHOTO BOOKS
Publishers of Fine Books in the Photographic Field
New York 10, N. Y.